Contents

Jobs

A I like being on my own

1 Vocabulary. Look at the box and find the word for a person who ...

1. builds houses.
   a builder
2. designs houses.
   an architect
3. grows food in his or her fields.
4. repairs cars.
5. repairs water pipes.
6. sells meat.
7. makes or sells bread.
8. sells vegetables.
9. works in an office and deals with correspondence, filing, etc.
10. cures sick animals.
11. looks after sick people.
12. repairs household machinery.
13. cooks in a hotel or restaurant.
14. looks after people's teeth.
15. flies aeroplanes.

> an architect   a baker   a builder   a butcher
> a chef   a dentist   a farmer   a greengrocer
> a mechanic   a nurse   a pilot   a plumber
> a secretary   a service engineer   a vet

2 Vocabulary. Write descriptions for these jobs.

1. a pianist
   a person who plays the piano
2. a barmaid or barman
   a person who works in a bar
3. a violinist
4. a bus driver
5. a forester
6. a broadcaster
7. an actor or actress
8. a journalist
9. an (air) steward or stewardess
10. a housewife
11. a policeman or policewoman
12. an electrician
13. a carpenter
14. a writer
15. a gardener

I CAN'T REMEMBER IF I'M GOING TO WORK OR JUST GETTING HOME!

3 Grammar revision. Make questions.

1. Tony Robinson's two sisters work in a bank.
   Where do Tony Robinson's two sisters work?
2. Basil Mulford lives in a small village. (*Where ...?*)
3. John Peake likes working outdoors. (*Where ...?*)
4. Tony does the ironing before breakfast. (*When ...?*)
5. Vera Hibbert usually has her lunch in the kitchen. (*Where ...?*)
6. The director of the car factory goes to work by Rolls-Royce. (*How ...?*)
7. Tom White looks like his mother's father. (*Who ...?*)
8. Mrs Cabeldu teaches the smallest children. (*Who ...?*)

469

The Cambridge English Course

We have not provided space for you
to write in this Practice Book,
except in the crosswords. Instead,
we have used the space to put in
more exercises.

3 Practice Book

Michael Swan and Catherine Walter

Cambridge University Press
Cambridge
New York   Port Chester   Melbourne   Sydney

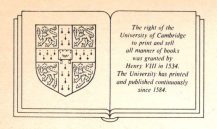

The right of the
University of Cambridge
to print and sell
all manner of books
was granted by
Henry VIII in 1534.
The University has printed
and published continuously
since 1584.

Published by the Press Syndicate of the University of Cambridge
The Pitt Building, Trumpington Street, Cambridge CB2 1RP
40 West 20th Street, New York, NY 10011, USA
10 Stamford Road, Oakleigh, Melbourne 3166, Australia

© Cambridge University Press 1988

First published 1988
Fourth printing 1989

Designed by Banks and Miles, London
Typeset by Text Filmsetters Ltd, London
Origination by C.S. Colour Ltd, London
Printed in Great Britain by Scotprint Ltd, Musselburgh, Scotland

ISBN 0 521 27878 3 Practice Book 3
ISBN 0 521 27879 1 Student's Book 3
ISBN 0 521 27877 5 Teacher's Book 3
ISBN 0 521 31627 8 Test Book 3
ISBN 0 521 26245 3 Cassette Set 3
ISBN 0 521 30325 7 Student's Cassette 3

4 Grammar revision. Make negative sentences.

1. Our cat likes fish. (*Our dog*)
   Our dog doesn't like fish.
2. Alice looks like her mother. (*Polly*)
3. People here usually work on Saturdays. (*Sundays*)
4. Wood floats. (*Iron*)
5. It rains a lot in Scotland. (*Tunisia*)

6. Eric can speak Spanish. (*Susan*)
7. There was a phone call for you. (*me*)
8. Most people of sixty look old. (*My father*)
9. The kitchen needs cleaning. (*The living room*)
10. The woman in the red coat comes to every meeting. (*blue*)

5 Read the following text, and then write two or three paragraphs about how you spend your day. Try to use all of the words and expressions in the box.

I am a commercial artist. Many people imagine that artists live a lazy life. Perhaps some do. However, my family get very bad-tempered if there is no food, and I find I have to work quite hard to pay the bills. So I do not simply sleep all morning, stagger out of bed at midday, and go off to the pub for a liquid breakfast. Here is how I spend my day.

I get up at about eight o'clock. I wash, dress, and have breakfast. I look through the mail, hoping to find cheques and commissions. There are never enough of either. When breakfast is over I drive to my studio and spend the morning working. Working, for me, means trying to think of new design ideas, and then working the ideas out in detail when I have found them. This goes on till about twelve-thirty or one o'clock; then I have a quick sandwich lunch, and after that it's back to work. During the afternoon I often have meetings with clients. These tend to be difficult, because many of my clients have strong views about art (although very few of them know what they are talking about). By the time five-thirty comes round I'm more than ready to stop. I close up the studio, drive home, and begin to relax.

after that	although	because	by the time	during	however
if	not simply	so	then	till	when	

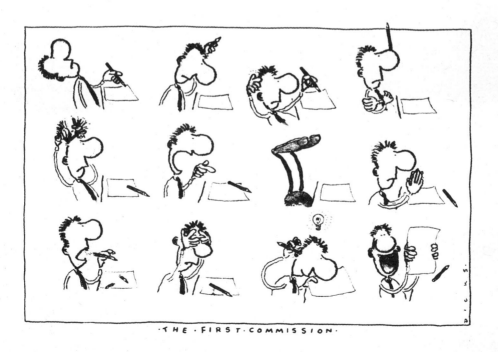

·THE·FIRST·COMMISSION·

5

6 Read one or both of these texts. You can use your dictionary if you wish.

WHAT IS HE?
What is he?
– A man, of course.
Yes, but what does he do?
– He lives and is a man.
Oh quite! but he must work. He must have a job of some sort.
– Why?
Because obviously he's not one of the leisured classes.
– I don't know. He has lots of leisure. And he makes quite beautiful chairs.
There you are then! He's a cabinet maker.
– No no!
Anyhow a carpenter and joiner.
– Not at all.
But you said so.
– What did I say?
That he made chairs, and was a joiner and carpenter.
– I said he made chairs, but I did not say he was a carpenter.
All right then, he's just an amateur.
– Perhaps! Would you say a thrush was a professional flautist, or just an amateur?
I'd say it was just a bird.
– And I say he is just a man.
All right! You always did quibble.

(D.H. Lawrence)

A TWELVE-YEAR-OLD SERVANT
I left school when I was twelve and I had to go into service. I went to a young couple who were farmers, and I had to live in. It was about fifteen miles from home and it seemed to me the back of beyond. It was a big rambling place, and I was the only help they had. I got one and threepence a week. They weren't bad to me, but they used to go out a lot and I'd be in the place on my own. I'd go and look in all the cupboards, under beds, I was literally terrified. I helped the mistress make butter, and sometimes I used to milk the cows as well. Anyway, I didn't last long. I got so lonely. I went to a butcher's wife near Wellingborough. She was a terror. There was another maid there, and fortunately we got on well together. We could laugh and cover up for each other if we did anything wrong. We slept in an attic, and we had to be up at six o'clock in the morning. If we were a minute or two late, she'd be there and want to know why. I reckon she laid awake all night long, just for the pleasure of catching us out in the morning.

I had fifteen places in twelve years, and only at one of them was I treated like a human being. They didn't think of us as people like themselves. We were different. Occasionally my father and brother used to come and see me, and I felt really unhappy when they left. I wanted to say 'Take me with you', but of course they couldn't. You had to work; your parents couldn't afford to keep you. Sometimes, if I'd been home, when the time came for me to go back I used to pray that the train wouldn't come or that it would crash. But it always came.

('Mrs Webb', from *Loneliness* by Jeremy Seabrook)

"I warn you, Smedley, these blasted daydreams have to stop!"

B I wander round the kitchen

1 Invent one or more completions for each of the following sentences. Use an *-ing* form in each sentence.

1. When I was a child, what I liked most about summer was . . .

   going barefoot.
   visiting my grandmother's farm.
2. . . . always reminds me of when we rode old Mr Fistner's horse, without a saddle.

   Seeing a white horse
   Talking about childhood summers
3. I was always a little afraid of . . .
4. It was . . . that my sister was afraid of.
5. But . . . made me feel brave and adventurous.
6. What my sister really loved was . . .
7. We were never satisfied with . . .
8. I always insisted on . . .
9. . . . was against my parents' rules, but we did it anyway when we thought they wouldn't find out.

Now look at the rules below, and try to say which of the nine sentences follows which rule.

A: *-ing* forms are used as subjects of sentences.
B: *-ing* forms are used after the verb *to be*.
C: *-ing* forms are used after prepositions.

2 Write down four things you like doing and four things you don't like doing. Then write a sentence about each one, saying what you like or dislike about it. Use the two forms you learnt in Lesson 1A. Examples:

What I like is being outdoors.
It's being too busy that I don't like.

3 Infinitive or *-ing* form? Choose the correct forms. If you are unsure, look at the rules on page 137, and write another sentence using the same verb followed by the correct form.

1. I try to avoid *working/to work* overtime.
2. Would you agree *working/to work* at the weekend once a month if you could have days off during the week?
3. My brother has asked *having/to have* a year's unpaid leave to work on a personal project.
4. Shelagh dislikes *having/to have* to train new secretaries so often, because as soon as they are trained they leave for better-paid jobs.
5. I don't know anybody who enjoys *filling in/to fill in* Value Added Tax forms.
6. I have just begun *understanding/to understand* how this organisation really works.
7. Some days I feel like *walking/to walk* out of my office and never *coming/to come* back.
8. Have you decided *accepting/to accept* the new job?
9. Excuse me a minute – I think I've forgotten *turning off/to turn off* my microcomputer.
10. Bill, my policeman friend, says he never has enough time to finish *doing/to do* his paperwork.
11. I can't imagine *working/to work* freelance – I don't think I'd have the discipline.
12. I happened *overhearing/to overhear* you – I think you'll work faster if you assemble the parts this way.
13. Do you mind *being/to be* away from your family on business trips so much?
14. Have you ever learnt *operating/to operate* a telex machine?
15. Mr Levin won't be in this week – I suggest *getting/to get* a temp to cover his workload.
16. I can't help *wondering/to wonder* who hired that man.
17. Did you manage *finding out/to find out* who was behind the decision?
18. She seems *liking/to like* the added responsibility her new job gives her.

4 Read the sentences and look at the diagrams.

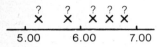

I'll arrive at 7.00.

I'll arrive by 7.00.

Now put *at* or *by* in each sentence.

1. This train is always exactly on time; it arrives .... 12.43 precisely.
2. I can't tell you exactly when I'll get there, but I promise I'll be there .... 6.00.
3. .... the time I've prepared breakfast, he's got the kids dressed.
4. I met Susan Sontag in Paris; .... the time I was working in an art gallery.
5. Why don't you phone me at 8.30 – I'll be home .... then.
6. Be sure and phone me .... 8.30 – that's when I have to leave for the station.
7. Veronica left the house .... 7.45 and walked directly to the shop.
8. The baby will probably be walking and talking .... the next time you come.

5 Spelling revision. Single or double letters?
Examples:

di(f)erent *different*

a(l)one *alone*

a(f)ord be(t)er bo(r)ing co(f)ee
coo(k)ing co(m)unist dre(s)ed fi(n)ish
fortunate(l)y iro(n)ing le(t)er ma(r)ied
mea(n)ing pa(r)ents po(s)ible pu(t)ing
si(t)ing usua(l)y wo(r)ied wri(t)er

6 Read the texts.

This is a story about four people named Everybody, Somebody, Anybody, and Nobody. There was an important job to be done and Everybody was asked to do it. Everybody was sure Somebody would do it. Anybody could have done it, but Nobody did it. Somebody got angry about that, because it was Everybody's job. Everybody thought Anybody could do it but Nobody realised that Everybody wouldn't do it. It ended up that Everybody blamed Somebody when Nobody did what Anybody could have done.

How much is the average British housewife worth? The answer is £370 a week. An insurance company has carried out a survey to find out the value of a housewife's work. It seems that she is on call for 92 hours in a seven-day week, working as a shopper, waitress, nurse, driver, cook, cleaner and child-minder. Taking employment agencies' standard fees for these jobs, the insurance company has calculated that a housewife's work is worth £19,753 a year – more than the salary of a bishop, a divisional fire service chief or a second division footballer.

7 Write about one of the following subjects. Use some words and expressions from Unit 1 of the Student's Book.

1. How do you spend your working day (now, in the past, or in your imagination)?
2. Would you work if you didn't need the money? If not, what would you do?
3. Would you like to live in the same way as Tony (Student's Book Lesson 1B, Exercise 2)? Why (not)?

"Miss Ellis, could you come in here and pass me my coffee?"

Unit 2

Wildlife

Ⓐ Every ten minutes

1 Vocabulary revision. Can you put the words with the right pictures? (Some words can be used more than once.)

bacon   beef   calf   cheese   chicken   cow   cream   egg   fur   ham   lamb   leather
milk   mutton   pig   pork   rabbit   sheep   sheepskin   veal   wool   yoghurt

1

2

3

4

5

6

7

8

2 Grammar revision. These irregular verbs come in Student's Book Lesson 2A. Can you copy and complete the table?

INFINITIVE	PAST	PARTICIPLE
beat	....	beaten
....	became	....
....	....	built
choose	....	....
....	did	....
....	....	found
get	....	....
....	gave	....
....	....	known
make	....	....
....	said	....
....	....	scnt
wake up	....	....

3 Pronunciation: stress. Practise saying these words. They are all stressed on the second part, like this: beLIEVE (/bɪ'li:v/).

believe   create   destroy   effect
extinct   provide   remain
surprised   survive

4 How do you feel about these statements? Write a few words giving your opinion about some of them. For example:

I agree strongly. ....   I have no view. ....
I agree. ....   I disagree. ....
It depends. ....   I disagree strongly. ....

1. Animals should not be kept in zoos.
2. It is wrong to hunt animals for sport.
3. People shouldn't buy clothes made of animal fur.
4. It is wrong to kill animals for food.
5. Hunting and fishing are good, natural sports.
6. Governments should spend more money to save rare animals that are in danger of becoming extinct.
7. Millions of people starve to death every year. Governments should spend less money on animals and more money on people.

5 Choose one of the statements from Exercise 4 and write more about what you think. Try to use some of these words.

alive	almost	chemical	create	death	destroy
earth	except	forest	hunt	in danger	
international	left	less	natural	nuclear	plant
rare	remain	save	successful	survive	

VETERINARIAN

N. Twohy

"My third husband was delicious."

6 Read this with a dictionary.

DID YOU KNOW?

A giraffe's heart weighs 22 kilos.

A grizzly bear can run as fast as a horse.

In a lion family, the females do more than 90% of the hunting.

The first camels lived in North America.

A new-born baby blue whale weighs as much as an adult African elephant.

In 1865, there were about 13 million bison (buffalo) in North America. In 1883 there were only a few hundred left.

A new-born panda is smaller than a mouse, and weighs about 100 grams.

Wolves never normally attack people. For years, a Canadian newspaper has offered a reward to anyone who could prove that a wolf had attacked a person; nobody has claimed the reward.

Wolves are monogamous, and they are devoted parents.

Wolves do not normally hunt in packs (though they may do so in winter).

Unit 2

B Bird, mammal, insect or tree?

1 Vocabulary. Use the numbered categories to classify the words and expressions in the box.

> animal   chase   chemical   continent
> destroy   disappearing   fur   gentle
> hunt   in danger   Mediterranean   neck
> nuclear   plant   rare   save   skin
> stomach

1. Kinds of poisons that go into the sea

   chemical , nuclear

2. Kinds of living things
3. Parts of animals
4. Geographical words
5. Words that could describe the oryx
6. Things you can do to an animal

"I'm sorry, sir – we don't do part exchange."

11

2 Do you know the difference? Fill the blanks; use a dictionary if you are not sure of your answers.

| average/normal   chasing/hunting   damaged/hurt   expensive/valuable   neck/throat |
| poem/poetry   rare/valuable |

1. The Indian elephant is a .... animal, and its tusks (its two long teeth) are very ....
2. The National Park wardens were .... some men who had been .... elephants for their tusks.
3. One of the elephants was ...., and when the wardens tried to get close to it, it .... their van.
4. I enjoy reading some kinds of ...., but I have never written a .... in my life.

5. I have an old book by the poet Blake; it was not very .... when my mother bought it, but it seems that it is extremely .... now.
6. If you have a cough and a sore ...., you shouldn't go out without covering your .... up well.
7. The .... person living in a big city gets far more coughs than if he or she lived in the country; so it's not .... to have as many coughs as most city-dwellers do.

3 Grammar revision. *Be* or *have*?

1. .... you hungry?
2. Phone for an ambulance – there .... been an accident.
3. My father .... nearly two metres tall.
4. What .... your new car like?

5. I .... thirsty – .... you got a drink?
6. .... you afraid of spiders?
7. I think I'm ill – I .... cold, but I .... a temperature.

4 Grammar: quantifiers. Put in words from the box, with or without *of*. (More than one answer may be possible.)

| all   nearly all   most   many   some   several   a few   not many   hardly any |
| no/none   any |

1. .... the grain farmers grow today is descended from wild species.
2. .... the farmers in this country care about plant and wild animal conservation.
3. .... kinds of wild mammals in France originally came from other countries.
4. Britain has very strict laws about bringing animals into the country, but every year .... people try to import animals illegally.

5. .... the medicines used today are derived from plants found in the tropical rain forest.
6. .... the world's fishing countries should agree to stop hunting whales.
7. Whale, rat, horse, cat, spider, sheep, crocodile, cow, snake, elephant, oryx, tiger, lizard: .... these animals are mammals and .... the others are reptiles.
8. .... hunters are interested in keeping .... wildlife alive and healthy.

"Well, at least we've got more room than the poor sods in the other tank."

5 Read one or both of these stories. Try to understand the story in each case by guessing the meanings of words you don't know. Then use your dictionary to see if you were right.

Tree talk about a plot to kill caterpillars

If the National Science Foundation and two scientists it supports with research money are to be believed, trees talk to each other.

At least they do in the woods near Seattle, where Drs Gordon Orians and David Rhoades of the University of Washington have found that the willows and the alders warn each other when they are being attacked by leaf-eating insects.

'I know it sounds like something right out of a comic strip, but it is definitely a form of communication we've witnessed in dozens and dozens of trees,' Dr Orians said.

'We cannot explain what happened without assuming that trees being damaged by insects release a chemical in the air that warns nearby undamaged trees to prepare a defence against these insects.'

About four years ago, Dr Orians and Dr Rhoades set out to find how trees survive mass attacks by insects such as tent caterpillars and webworms.

The two ecologists placed swarms of as many as 700 tent caterpillars and webworms in the branches of willows and alders.

The trees being attacked began producing chemicals such as alkaloids and terpenoids.

'The insects began to lose all their vitality,' Dr Orians said.

(from an article by Thomas O'Toole in *The Guardian*)

A new branch of ant learning

Seeing ants gather around the early broad beans is not a sight to gladden the amateur gardener. For the ants are there because tiny aphids have arrived earlier. Aphids feed on the plant sap, and they produce a kind of nectar which the ants collect and carry off to their underground nests. Everybody wins – except the plants.

But scientists at Cornell University in New York have been investigating another case of ant–plant behaviour where both sides come out winning. It is described as 'mutualism', a state in which both plant and insect derive benefit from the other. The plant, a tropical shrub, has the ability to produce globular food bodies – comfortable ant-sized meals – on the interior of hollow stems. The stems make a cosy home for the ants, while the ants defend the plant against the hordes of other insects which would otherwise consume it. This

seems a sensible and beneficial relationship.

But there is a twist to the tale or at least to its biochemistry. In some way, as yet not defined, the plant knows when the ants arrive to colonise its attractive apartments. When the ants are not there, it produces no food for them. When they are there it produces food in abundance. How does the plant know when the ants are there?

(from an article by Anthony Tucker in *The Guardian*)

Interests

A Art, bird-watching, cars, dancing, . . .

1 Vocabulary. Can you match words from the two lists? Example:

cooking – saucepan

art   bird-watching   cooking   the countryside   dancing   drawing   driving   gardening
history   jazz   opera   reading   shooting   sport   swimming   theatre   travel

aria   canvas   crawl   cup final   eagle   footpath   lawnmower   Middle Ages   novel
partner   pencil   petrol consumption   saucepan   saxophone   shotgun   stage   suitcase

2 Grammar revision. Put in *a(n)* or *the* if necessary.

1. She wants to be ...*an*... architect.
2. What's ...*the*... time?
3. I like ....⌐.... music.
4. 'What's your husband interested in?' '..........
   cars and .... money.'
5. I went to get .... photos, but they weren't ready.
6. 'Who broke the window?' 'I don't know. Somebody threw .... stone at it.'
7. 'Do you know .... people in .... house next door?' 'Not very well.'
8. .... food is really expensive these days.
9. My daughter wants to study .... engineering at university.
10. Would you like .... drink?
11. I can remember .... faces, but I can never remember .... names.
12. 'Can I borrow your car?' 'Yes, sure. Here are .... keys.'

3 Grammar revision. Write true answers to each sentence, as in the example. Use *So am I, So do I, So can I* etc., and *I'm not, I don't* etc.

1. I'm tired.
   So am I.   OR   I'm not.
2. I was in France last summer.
3. I used to get more exercise than I do now.
4. I've got a colour television.
5. I believe that you can sometimes communicate your thoughts to another person.
6. When I was a child, I thought people on television could see me.
7. I can speak a few words of Japanese.
8. I'll speak English much better by this time next year.

Now write answers about your family and friends, as in the examples.

9. My mother was very politically active when she was younger.
   So was my mother. OR So was mine.
   OR So was my aunt.
   OR My mother wasn't.
10. My mother was always very tired in the evenings.
11. My father used to tell us bedtime stories almost every night.
12. My husband has got a good sense of humour.
13. My little nephew believes in ghosts.
14. My family lived in a very small village when I was a child.
15. My sister can play the piano beautifully.
16. My brother will be a terrific father.

"Lord! I hope you win after all this practice!"

14

4 Grammar revision. Write five or more things that you used to do when you were a child. Example:

I used to go skating in winter.

5 Write about your past and present interests. What were you interested in when you were a child? What did you want to do in life? How much have your interests changed? What are your present ambitions?

6 Look quickly at the three texts. Choose the one that looks most interesting and read it (using a dictionary if you want to). Then write two or three sentences, explaining why you chose the text, whether you found it interesting or not, and why.

"Don't worry, the wife won't be back from her macramé, or origami, or whatever the hell she's studying these days."

Commuter who talks to strangers!

Peter Lloyd does something extraordinary on the Underground each day – he talks to total strangers.

He struck up his first conversation four weeks ago and found that people actually enjoyed talking.

Peter is now London's leading Tube talker, dedicated to converting a silent public to the joys of a nice chat.

He followed up the first experimental chat with a letter published in *The Evening Standard*, announcing the Tube Talker project.

The project is still in the discussion stage, but Peter is considering membership cards on which people would pledge their support for Tube talking and even a newsletter with accounts of interesting chats.

Most of all he wants London Transport to designate some Tube carriages as compartments where talking is encouraged.

Peter, a 24-year-old personnel consultant, is quite serious about his plans and has won some converts.

'People often look so sad and lonely on the Tube,' he said. 'They're usually pleased when I break the ice.'

(The Evening Standard)

What are his intentions?

DEAR ABBY: My daughter met a smooth-talking fellow nine months ago and really fell for him. She's 22 and he's 21. He isn't working now and he's not even looking. He keeps saying that the jobs he wants don't pay enough. In the meantime he borrows from my daughter, drives her car, eats every meal at my table, and his clothes are washed in my machine! He never mentions marriage, but my daughter looks at him like he's a god, and she calls this 'love'.

Would I be wrong to ask this guy what his intentions are?
– FED UP

DEAR FED UP: You can ask him, but I think I can tell you. His intentions are to eat at your table, drive your daughter's car, get his clothes washed in your machine, and freeload off you and your daughter as long as you let him.

(The Houston Post)

First US city to be bombed from the air

In 1921, during one of the worst race riots in American history, Tulsa, Okla., became the first US city to be bombed from the air. More than 75 persons – mostly blacks – were killed.

Before the riot, Tulsa blacks were so successful that their business district was called 'The Negro's Wall Street'. Envy bred hatred of the blacks, who accounted for a tenth of the segregated city's population of 100,000.

Then on May 30, 1921, a white female elevator operator accused Dick Rowland, a 19-year-old black who worked at a shoeshine stand, of attacking her. Though he denied the charge, Rowland was jailed. The Tulsa *Tribune* ran a sensational account of the incident the next day, and a white lynch mob soon gathered at the jail. Armed blacks, seeking to protect Rowland, also showed up. Someone fired a gun, and the riot was on.

Whites invaded the black district, burning, looting and killing. To break up the riot, the police commandeered private planes and dropped dynamite. Eventually, the National Guard was called in and martial law declared.

The police arrested more than 4,000 blacks and interned them in three camps. All blacks were forced to carry green ID cards. And when Tulsa was zoned for a new railroad station, the tracks were routed through the black business district, thus destroying it.

(Parade Magazine)

B I told you a bit of a lie

1 Vocabulary revision. Put the words with the right pictures.

cooker   dishwasher   dryer   food processor   fridge   hairdryer
headphones   heater   home computer   lawnmower
personal stereo   power tool   toaster   TV   video   washing machine

2 Stress. Practise pronouncing these words from Exercise 1.

fridge   cooker   TV
             dryer
             heater
             toaster
             headphones

dishwasher   washing machine
hairdryer   home computer
lawnmower   food processor
power tool   personal stereo
video

3 Grammar revision. Join the sentences using a possessive *'s* or *s'*.

1. Phil has a sports car. It can do 180 kph.

   Phil's sports car can do 180 kph.

2. My parents live on a farm. It's near the Canadian border.

   My parents' farm is near the Canadian border.

3. Mr Shephard uses a computer. It saves him a lot of time.
4. Jake has got a new job. It seems to be very interesting.
5. The girls have music lessons. They're on Mondays.
6. Alice Benson has written a novel. It's not very good.
7. The management has made a new offer. It's too low, so we're going to strike.
8. The children have got a room on the first floor. It's always in a mess.
9. My dentist has got a new receptionist. She's really beautiful.
10. The dogs were barking last night. It woke me up.

4 Imagine. Write sentences beginning with *if*, as in the example.

1. Imagine you were a millionaire.

   If I were a millionaire, I'd stop working and move to Barbados.

2. Imagine you could communicate with animals.
3. Imagine the government of your country disappeared overnight.
4. Imagine men could have babies.
5. Imagine you could communicate your thoughts to other people.
6. Imagine there were no more illness on the earth.
7. Imagine you didn't feel it when you hurt yourself.
8. Imagine all weapons disappeared from the earth.
9. Imagine everyone on the earth spoke a common language.
10. Imagine there were no more advertising.
11. Imagine you could breathe under water.
12. Imagine you could fly.
13. Imagine there were no aeroplanes, telephones or televisions.
14. Imagine paper became very, very expensive.

5 Read the first text. Then copy and complete the second text, using the information in the box and the vocabulary in the first text.

Neville and Rachel are happily married, and they get on well together, but they are very different kinds of people. Rachel is a cheerful outgoing woman who enjoys talking to people; Neville is very reserved, though he likes the company of his friends.

Rachel is interested in sport – especially tennis and swimming – while Neville is more of an indoor type who prefers reading and listening to music. Neville likes cooking, and makes delicious meals for the family; Rachel can't stand housework.

However, in spite of their differences, they do have one thing in common: they are both gifted and enthusiastic photographers, and they have organised several successful exhibitions of their work.

Anne and Peter are very similar .... people. They are both rather ...., ... they enjoy the .... of their friends. They .... like sport, ... ball games: Anne plays .... regularly, while Peter plays .... for his local club.

Anne and Peter are .... very .... in .... music, and they often go to concerts. .... is a good violinist; .... doesn't play an instrument. Neither of them can .... music.

However, ... of all the things they have in ...., they do not always .... very well together, and they are not really very .... married.

	ANNE	PETER
PERSONALITY:	reserved	reserved
GAMES:	basketball	football
	tennis	
INSTRUMENTS:	violin	none
CLASSICAL MUSIC:	likes	likes
POP MUSIC:	hates	hates

6 Write a comparison of yourself and another person, saying what you have in common and what the differences are.

7 Read this with a dictionary.

STRANGE BUT TRUE
Bamboo can grow 1 metre in 24 hours.
Napoleon was afraid of cats.
There were elephants, lions and camels in Alaska 12,000 years ago.
In the winters of 1420 and 1438, wolves were found in the streets of Paris.
If all the ice in the world melted, the sea would rise over 50 metres.
85% of all the world's plants grow in the sea.
Reykjavik, the capital of Iceland, is heated by underground hot springs.

Nearly 25% of the surface of Los Angeles is occupied by cars.
99% of all the forms of life that have ever existed on the earth are now extinct.
All US Presidents have worn glasses.
35% of all Americans are overweight.
Your skin weighs nearly three kilograms.
The first parachute jump was made by a dog in a basket (belonging to the French balloonist Blanchard) in 1785.
Betsy, a chimpanzee at the Baltimore zoo, paints pictures, and has had 65 of them sold.
The most common name in the world is Muhammad.

(Information taken from *The Book of Facts* by Isaac Asimov)

Unit 4

Getting what you want

A Nice woman, 42

1 Put in words from the box.

advertisements   advertising   afford   bargains   cheap   cheaper   choice   easy
economists   else   enjoy   expensive   furious   interrupted   magazines   need
posters   quality   queuing   sales   series   small ads   spending

I hate .....1...... It annoys me when I'm watching TV and a good film is .....2..... every twenty minutes or so by a .....3..... of eight or ten stupid lying commercials – I always turn the sound off. I never look at newspaper .....4....., and I don't even open the kind of glossy .....5..... where there is more advertising than anything .....6...... And it makes me really .....7..... when I see .....8..... all over the place trying to persuade me to make somebody else rich by .....9..... money I can't .....10... on things I don't .....11...., especially when half the world is starving.

Just now the shops are having .....12..... There are advertisements everywhere offering magnificent .....13...., and people are .....14.... up for days in advance, just so that they can be first

into the shop when the sale starts. I'd rather stay at home, put my feet up and .....15.... what I've got.

.....16.... tend to argue that if we didn't have advertising there wouldn't be such a wide .....17.... of things to buy. Perhaps, but I think advertising makes things more .....18...., and it would be better if the money were spent on improving .....19.... or making things .....20.....

.....21.... are different, perhaps. I think they perform a useful service, because they put individual buyers and sellers in direct contact. You can find things you really need – like a .....22.... second-hand car being offered directly by the owner – and if you want to sell something yourself a small ad is an .....23.... way of getting rid of it.

"We have high quality and low prices. Which do you want?"

2 Grammar revision. Put in the subject and a present progressive verb.

1. What .... this evening? (*you and your sister; do*)

   What are you and your sister doing this evening?

2. What time .... tomorrow? (*Malcolm and Virginia; arrive*)
3. What school .... now? (*Hannah's two children; go to*)
4. Where .... these days? (*you and your karate class; meet*)
5. .... again? (*it; rain*)
6. Why ....? (*that woman in the red coat; cry*)
7. Where .... for her holiday this year? (*that teacher friend of yours – what's her name, Jill? – ; go*)
8. .... yet? (*the kettle; boil*)
9. .... really ...., or was it just a rumour? (*John and Susan; get divorced*)
10. .... still .... pigeons? (*your friend Yvonne and her husband; breed*)

3 Grammar revision. Choose the correct tense: simple present or present progressive.

1. 'Hello, Alec. What .... these days?' (*do you do / are you doing*)
2. 'Well, just now I .... to classes in computer programming and German, believe it or not. (*go / 'm going*)
3. In my business, most people .... at least two languages. (*speak / are speaking*)
4. And everybody .... computers the whole time. (*uses / is using*)
5. You know our factory .... central heating systems. (*produces / is producing*)
6. Well, we .... a new type of boiler that is 30% more efficient. (*just develop / are just developing*)
7. I .... to Switzerland next week for discussions with Head Office about prices. (*fly / am flying*)
8. It's difficult. Costs of raw materials .... steadily higher. (*get / are getting*)
9. And of course labour .... more than anything else.' (*always costs / is always costing*)

4 Which sentences are right?

1. She shoulds see a doctor.
   She should see a doctor.
2. Might she listen to me?
   Do she might listen to me?
3. You can't be serious!
   You don't can be serious!
4. You must have forgotten what she said yesterday.
   You must to have forgotten what she said yesterday.
5. How did I should answer?
   How should I have answered?
6. I'd like to can help her.
   I'd like to be able to help her.

The verbs in the sentences above are called 'modal' verbs, and they work by special rules. Can you fill in the blanks in the rules?

FOR MODALS:
1. There is .... in the third person singular of the present tense.
2. Other auxiliary verbs (like *do* or *did*) are ....
3. The verb form that follows a modal is ....

5 Look at the picture and draw some conclusions about the person who lives in this room. Write at least eight sentences.

The person must speak English.
He or she might have a motorbike.

6 Read some or all of the sections of the advertisement on the opposite page. Read through once trying to understand without using a dictionary. Then read again using a dictionary to check whether your guesses were right.

SOME OF THE GREATEST BUSINESS DEALS OF ALL TIME

1. The Red Indian dope trick

Even in the days when America was known as the New World, it was a country with a reputation for its spirit of enterprise and the ability of its people to make a good deal.

When the settlers started negotiating, the natives hardly knew what had hit them – and in the summer of 1626, probably the most spectacular real estate coup in history took place.

Governor Peter Minuit of the Dutch West India Company had the job of buying Manhattan Island from the Indians.

After some haggling with Chief Manhasset, the price was agreed at 24 dollars' worth of kettles, axes and cloth.

Today, $24 would not buy one square foot of office space in New York City, and an office block in central Manhattan changes hands for around $80 million. Even allowing for inflation, Minuit got himself a real bargain.

2. Not again, Josephine!

You would think that the Manhattan deal would remain a one-off for ever. After all, the Americans would surely never find anyone as naive as the Indian chief again.

But less than two centuries later, they did – and this time the loser was Napoleon, Emperor of France and (in his early years, at least) a brilliant military tactician.

In 1803, Napoleon had his mind on European affairs (in particular, an invasion of Britain), so he decided to dispense with France's American possessions.

He sold the entire Mississippi valley, an area of 828,000 square miles extending from Canada down to the Gulf of Mexico and westwards to the Rockies, for just over 27 million dollars.

Through this deal, known as the Louisiana purchase, President Thomas Jefferson doubled the size of the United States for only around 5 cents per acre.

The judgement of the Emperor, on the other hand, never seemed to be quite the same again.

3. Striking a bargain

Just occasionally, however, the seller does come out of a clever business deal on top – as in this example of a man who sold an idea to a manufacturing company.

The particular beauty of this deal lies in the fact that the idea was not one which he could put into practice himself.

He simply approached a leading match company and offered to tell them how they could save thousands of pounds by means of one change to their manufacturing procedures. The change would cost absolutely nothing to carry out – but he would require a substantial percentage of the savings in return for the idea.

Not surprisingly, the match company were more than a little suspicious, and turned him down. After all, if this idea was so obvious to an outsider, surely they could work it out for themselves.

They duly went through the whole factory with a fine tooth-comb – but found nothing. By this time, they were so intrigued by the man's offer that they went back to him and agreed that if he could save them money, he could have the cut he wanted.

"Just put one striking surface on each matchbox instead of two," he advised them. "You'll cut the money you spend on abrasives by 50%."

They did – and they did. And over the next few years, the man who sold them the idea made a small fortune.

4. A horse in a Million

In 1978, the American bicycle importer Sam Rubin bought a 3-year-old racehorse for $25,000.

There didn't seem to be anything remarkable about John Henry at the time, and his previous owner was certainly satisfied with the amount, as he had bought the horse for only $1,100 as a yearling.

In 1980, however, John Henry suddenly blossomed and won $925,000 in prize money.

Then in 1981, he won the inaugural Arlington Million and became America's Horse of the Year. By the time he picked up the title for a second time in 1984, he had won the Million again, the Santa Anita Handicap twice, the Jockey Gold Cup, the Ballantine's Scotch Classic and a staggering $6,591,860 – almost twice as much as any other horse in world racing history.

Sam Rubin can have only one regret about his horse, and that is that he has no stud value at all. Unfortunately for him, John Henry is a gelding.

5. PC Tips

The example of John Henry proves that outstanding opportunities do still exist – and without doubt, the best deal in office computers at the moment is the Epson PC+.

The PC+ is every bit as powerful as the industry standard computer, and just as flexible.

It will run all of the huge amount of software designed for IBM PCs (plus, of course, Epson's own famous Taxi system) and will fit happily into any existing IBM network.

However, it can run the software over three times faster – and it takes an even greater range of printers and peripherals.

Furthermore, it is only three-quarters the size, is considerably easier to use and is absolutely packed with extra features. In fact, it has more built in as standard than any other PC on the market.

As you would expect of an Epson, the PC+ is also exceptionally reliable.

Yet for all this, it costs an astonishing 25% less than the industry standard.

To find out more about this extraordinary deal, either: write to Epson (U.K.) Limited, Freepost, Birmingham B37 5BR; call up Prestel *280#; or dial 100 and ask for Freefone Epson.

It may differ from the previous four deals in that more than one party can benefit from it – but that doesn't mean you should waste any time in taking advantage.

(Epson advertisement, 1986)

1

Unit 4

B I've run out of soap

1 Grammar: verbs with two objects. Change the sentences as in the examples.

1. Can you get some stamps for me?

   Can you get me some stamps?
2. I ordered a steak for Mary.

   I ordered Mary a steak.
3. John bought some flowers for his mother.
4. They've sent the wrong bill to me again.
5. Don't give any more beer to Richard.
6. You'd better write a letter to the manager.
7. I've bought a present for you.
8. I'm going to tell the whole story to the police.
9. Veronica taught a song to us.
10. Don't ever offer a cigar to Al.
11. Bob made a lovely cake for us.
12. I'll never do a favour for Jane again.
13. I wonder if you could pass the spinach to me?
14. Has Bill shown the kitchen plans to you yet?
15. Never tell a bigger lie to anybody than you think they'll believe.
16. I wonder if you could take this book to Helen when you next go to London?
17. Could you bring a clean fork for me, please? This one is dirty.

2 Put in suitable words (you may need to put in more than one word).

1. '............ some tea?' 'Yes, ... love some.'
2. '............ I give you a .... with the washing up?' 'That's .... of you.'
3. 'I've .... out of stamps. .... I borrow some from you?' 'I'm .... I haven't got ....?'
4. '............ you mind telling me your name?' 'Andrew.'
5. '............ you hungry?' 'No, but .... like a drink of water, if you wouldn't ....'
6. '............ come out with us at the weekend?' 'That .... very nice. Thank you.'
7. '............ a light?' '............ have a look.'

3 Vocabulary. What are these?

1. a thing for keeping the rain off
2. stuff that you wash with
3. a pointed thing that you write with
4. a thing with a handle that you open to get into a room
5. a thing that goes on top of a box or tin
6. liquid that you can put in coffee
7. a round thing that you use to direct a car with
8. a thing that hangs from the ceiling and gives out light
9. a thing that you pick up when you want to talk to people who are a long way away
10. a machine that keeps things cold
11. a thing with a handle at one end that you use for cutting
12. a thing with three or four points that you put food into your mouth with

4 Vocabulary. Write descriptions (like the ones in Exercise 3) of:

a coffee-pot   a toothbrush   a newspaper
a radio   a basket   a jacket   glue
olive oil   salt   grass

5 Write about one of the following subjects. Use some words and expressions from Unit 4 of the Student's Book.

1. Do you think advertising is a good or a bad thing? Why?
2. Have you ever had a problem because you didn't know how to say something in a foreign language? If so, tell the story.
3. Write three small ads, or design one big advertisement, for things that you want to sell.

22

6 Read some of these advertisements with a dictionary.

Will the parents of the boy who gave a little boy an apple in exchange for his tricycle outside the Sale Lido on Friday between 6 and 7, kindly return it at once?

(*The Manchester Evening News*)

FOR SALE. Steel Car Box Trailer. Ideal for dogs or musicians.

(*The Cork Examiner*)

NANYUKI farmer seeks lady with tractor with view to companionship and possibly marriage. Send picture of tractor. Littlewood, Box 132, Nanyuki.

(*The East African Standard*)

YOUNG BUSINESS GIRL would like another girl to share her furnished apartment. Must squeeze toothpaste from the bottom. Write Miss F.G., Box 440, Benington, Vermont.

(*The Benington Evening Banner*)

INFORMATION WANTED. Dr Ingram F. Anderson is interested to hear from anyone who knows of any silent films featuring Caruso singing.

(*The Gramophone*)

Odd-sized feet. Man with odd-sized feet, right foot 6½–7, left foot 8½–9 wishes to contact someone with similar problem but preferably with shoe sizes reversed with view to joint buying.

(*The South Wales Echo*)

FOR SALE, Twin beds: one hardly used.

(*The Kentish Express*)

PLEASE NOTE: You can order our rings by post. State size, or enclose string tied round finger.

(*Advert in Yorkshire paper*)

SITUATION WANTED. Keen but out of work actor looking for non-appearing, non-speaking parts.

(*The West Highland Free Press*)

WHY BREAK YOUR CHINA WASHING UP? Do it automatically in a dishwasher! From John R. Fordham, Epping. 'Phone 33. Established 1923.

(*The Surrey Mirror*)

HAIRCUTTING WHILE YOU WAIT

(*Notice in Dublin barber's*)

Hand your luggage to us.

WE WILL SEND IT IN ALL DIRECTIONS.

(*Tokyo forwarding agency*)

26th October

R.D. SMITH has one Sewing Machine for sale. Phone 66598 after 7 p.m. and ask for Mrs. Kelly who lives with him cheap.

27th October

R.D. SMITH informs us he has received several annoying telephone calls because of an incorrect ad. in yesterday's paper. It should have read: R.D. Smith has one sewing machine for sale. Cheap. Phone 66598 after 7 p.m. and ask for Mrs. Kelly who loves with him.

28th October

R.D. SMITH. We regret an error in R.D. Smith's classified advertisement yesterday. It should have read: R.D. Smith has one Sewing Machine for sale. Cheap. Phone 66598 and ask for Mrs. Kelly who lives with him after 7 p.m.

(*The Tanganyika Standard*)

HOW DARE THEY!

If you see an advertisement in the press, in print, on posters or a cinema commercial which makes you angry, write to us at the address below. (TV and radio commercials are dealt with by the I.B.A.)

The Advertising Standards Authority. ✓

ASA Ltd . Brook House, Torrington Place, London WC1E 7HN

7 Try the crossword.

ACROSS

1. When there are changes to be made at work, my boss always talks to me before taking a ....

8. Tony likes being .... his own.

9. This has to be done in every home in the world.

12. Running a home and raising children is a difficult ....

13. What do you want to .... when you grow up?

15. In good physical condition.

17. This box is really heavy. Can you give me a ....?

18. I'd rather not come quite so early, if .... wouldn't mind.

19. Not difficult.

20. I think we .... time having too many meetings at the office.

21. I once .... a job with another person – he came in the mornings and I came in the afternoons.

22. While you're up, could you .... me another serving spoon, please?

23. There were times when I thought my son would never grow ....

24. I .... more money now than I ever have, but I always seem to spend it all.

26. One way to keep fit.

28. I would love to be .... my own more often.

29. 'Is 7.30 all right?' 'Perfect. See you ....'

30. George wants to get fit, but he gets tired easily and finds it hard to keep up an exercise programme. Is he tough?

31. Very few people can .... to buy Rolls-Royces.

32. Ms Rankin started thinking of setting up her own business .... working for the Manson Forbes Company.

33. Shelagh works very hard, ... she's not very organised.

DOWN

2. Like.

3. She couldn't get a job in Leeds, ... she moved to Brighton.

4. '............. no! They've sent the wrong books!'

5. Is *save* the same as *spend*?

6. How old will you .... in the year 2000?

7. An unemployed person doesn't have one.

8. All right.

10. I wouldn't like to .... an office with Jim – he talks too much.

11. Chris and his wife are very different, but they seem to have a good ....

14. Did Jill .... whether she had found the mirror she was looking for?

16. Workers sometimes join one, so they can have more power when they disagree with their boss (*two words*).

20. I + you.

21. Where are you going to .... the Christmas holidays?

22. One way of getting something that isn't yours.

25. Not square, not triangular, not rectangular.

27. I try to .... a certain amount of money every month.

29. Not this.

(*Solution on page 137.*)

Crime and punishment

A What are prisons for?

1 Vocabulary. Copy and complete the vocabulary network, using some of the words in the list to help you. You can add to the network if you want.

catch   cheap   criminal
deterrent   guilt   prison
protection   punishment
rehabilitation   sentence
society

CRIME

people (and what they do)

.... (commits crime)

police (................)

jury* (decide on ....)

judge* (decides on ....)

fine

probation

reasons

advantages

*You can look these words up in the dictionary if you want to.

25

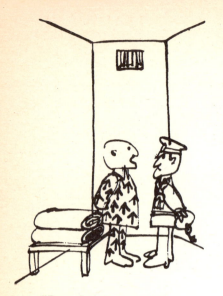

*"Permission to move my
cell around, sir?"*

2 Copy the sentences and underline the stressed syllables.

1. What are you doing these days?
2. Would you like some cheese?
3. That would be very nice.
4. I'm afraid Mary's not at home just now.
5. I'll wait till she comes back.
6. Can I talk to you for a minute?
7. Excuse me, have you got the time?
8. I wouldn't do that if I were you.
9. There are some men in the garden.
10. What shall we do?

3 Revision. Write the contracted forms. Example:

cannot *can't*

I have   she will   we would   they are
Sharon is   Sharon has   are not   is not
will not   have not   has not   could not
must not   should not   might not
were not   was not   had not

4 Revision. Write the plurals. Example:

person *people*

child   foot   man   mouse   sheep
tooth   woman   bus   baby   country
day   half   knife   watch

5 Read the tapescripts from the Student's Book lesson.

Tapescript for Exercise 3
'What is prison for, in your opinion?'
'Punishment.'
'Rehabilitation of offenders.'
'Somewhere to put people that we don't know what else to do with.'
'To remove criminals from society.'
'As a punishment and a deterrent.'
'A place to put people who don't conform.'

Tapescript for Exercise 4

FRANCES
Actually, it doesn't do any good, it doesn't deter cri- it doesn't stop crime, doesn't deter people from committing crime, and it costs society a lot of money to keep them there, between three and four hundred pounds a week . . . What deters people from committing crimes is the thought that they're actually going to get caught. Only 15, about 15% of crimes are cleared up in Britain. That means 85% of the crimes that are committed are not cleared up. So people think they're not going to get caught.

NICK
Well, I mean, the statistics about prison are something like, 82% of first-time offenders in prison go back to prison. So – you know, as far as the statistics go, no. And in fact my own personal experience, I learnt, you know, er, my offending got worse, got more and more serious . . . and I was doing bigger crimes and you know copping bigger sentences.

PENNY

I think that although some lip-service is paid to prison being rehabilitative, that actually it is a straight punishment . . . By and large in prison you sit and mark time, you have lost your job, you may well lose your family, you may well lose your accommodation while you're there, and you quite frequently come out knowing a lot more about how to break the law, and with a lot less reason not to do it again, because you've lost all the other things in the community that keep you from doing it in the first place, so I actually have a fairly negative view overall of what prison does.

Tapescript for Exercise 5

FRANCES

We have conditions which are appalling. Cockroaches and rats, we have three or four people banged up together with no sanitation . . . food is bad, there's no e-, very little, sometimes very little exercise or education – the conditions are absolutely appalling. They are barbaric and cruel.

NICK

I get really tired of some people who say prison is too soft. Prison is not soft at all . . . But the thing that hurts for me in prison – and also talking to other people – the main thing that hurt was that I didn't have my liberty. I couldn't just say you know, OK, I'm going to go for a walk now, I'm going to go out and see some friends of mine, or I want to do this – I couldn't do that. That's what hurts in prison . . . Days don't vary in prison . . . Something you don't get in prison is surprises. Very few surprises. You might get a visit you didn't think you'd get . . . And what I suddenly realised one day is that when you're in prison you only – you can only focus on the outside. That's where your focus is at. Right. Now – so, it's easy to assume that people on the outside, you are the main focus for them, but in fact you're not, because in the big wide world there's so much more going on. So, like, you know, people don't constantly think about you all the time. So of course when you don't get a letter when you think you should get one, it's very easy to get into 'people don't love me any more, I'm being rejected'.

"Don't worry, Winthrop, he won't get far."

6 Write 200 words or more on one of these subjects.

1. More attention should/shouldn't be given to how criminals can pay their victims back for the losses they have suffered.
2. Criminals' wives, husbands, and small children should/shouldn't be allowed to spend, for example, one weekend a month with them.
3. How the prison system should be changed.

B Danger – little old ladies!

1 Grammar. Make a story with the pictures, using '*If . . . hadn't . . . , . . . wouldn't have . . .*' Example:

If she hadn't robbed the bank, she wouldn't have had lunch in that restaurant.

1   2   3   4

5   6   7   8

2 Make up your own story using '*If . . . had(n't) . . . , . . . would(n't) have . . .*' Write at least five sentences, and use two of the pictures in each sentence.

3 Vocabulary revision. Which words and expressions go with which person? Write a list for each person. Then choose one person and write a description of him or her.

beard   big nose   black hair   fair hair
glasses   good-looking   grey hair
heavily built   long face   long hair
medium height   moustache   plain
round face   short   short hair   slim   tall
wrinkles

1   2   3   4

4 How honest are you? Answer each question 'Yes', 'No', or 'Perhaps'.

1. A shop assistant is very unhelpful and disagreeable to you. Then, when you are paying for the goods you have chosen, she makes a mistake and charges you £10 less than the real price. Do you tell her?
2. You find a wallet containing £200, with a name in it but no address. Do you take it to the police?
3. You drop and break your new camera. As you often travel for your work, you know that the insurance will pay for the camera if you say it was stolen while you were travelling. Do you say it was stolen?
4. One of your friends collects unusual ashtrays. You are dining at an expensive restaurant which has very beautiful ashtrays. Do you slip one into your briefcase?
5. Someone you like very much has been in China for the past six weeks. Your boss has an outside line on her telephone, and the calls are not recorded. She leaves you alone in the office for an hour. Do you phone your friend?
6. You are going through customs in a foreign country. The customs officer says that it is against the law for you to bring so much cash into the country; but hints that if you give him £10 he will pretend not to notice. Do you give him the bribe?
7. You are moving to another town and selling your house. You have agreed verbally to sell it to one person, but no papers have been signed. Another person offers you £2,000 more. Do you sell to the second person?
8. You break a glass while washing up alone in the kitchen at a friend's house. Do you put it in the bin and cover it up so no one will see it?

Scoring: Give yourself no points for each 'Yes', one point for each 'Perhaps' and two points for each 'No'. If your total score is between 11 and 16, you are very honest; if it is between 5 and 10, you are not quite honest; between 1 and 4, honesty is not very important to you; 0, people should count their fingers after they shake hands with you.

5 Imagine you are one of the little old ladies in Exercises 1 and 2 in Student's Book Lesson 5B. Write a letter to your favourite grandchild describing the incident and how you felt about it.

6 Choose three or more of these texts to read.
You can use your dictionary.

BACK TO EARTH

In July 1980, a Los Angeles truck driver took to the air in a deck chair attached to 42 weather balloons. He was fined $1,500 for failing to file a flight plan and for not having a license to fly balloons.

(*The Chilton Herald*)

Good Excuse For Speeding

INDIANAPOLIS (UPI) – A driver who claimed he was driving too fast because he was trying to kill a bee has won an award for his arresting officer for offering the most creative excuse for speeding in Indiana.

The Police League of Indiana on Thursday awarded the prize to Marion County Sherriff's Lt. Lee Hyland, who told of stopping the speeder.

Hyland, who heads Marion County's traffic control division, said the driver claimed he was allergic to bees and was afraid of the stinging insects.

The lieutenant said the driver even offered a dead bee as evidence – but Hyland noticed it had dust on its wings.

"The guy admitted he had been carrying that bee around in his pocket for months in case he ever got stopped," Hyland said.

The driver, who was not named, told Hyland the story had worked in the past. Hyland gave him a speeding ticket.

The league chose from more than 150 entries from across the state.

Robert Williams, league president and a Shelbyville police detective, awarded Hyland a police scanner for relating "the most humorous" excuse.

(*The Mainichi Daily News*, Tokyo)

Prisoner's night out starts ministry inquiry

By Richard Ford

A Home Office inquiry has started into how a prisoner at Brixton prison, south London, was able to have a night out visiting public houses and clubs.

The prisoner was discovered so drunk that he could not climb a rope hanging over a low wall to get back in the prison after an evening out. He was caught when a prison officer living in a house nearby saw him attempting to scale the wall.

Thinking a prison escape might be imminent, the officer called the police, who found the prisoner trying to climb back over the wall.

An investigation will be held to discover if other prisoners have been out "on the town". A Home Office Official said: "We are attempting to find out if this is more widespread and the prison governor is looking at security arrangements."

The prisoner was one of several who are considered "low risk" and work in the kitchens. They sleep in a dormitory which is near the main prison and is not surrounded by a high wall.

Since the prisoner was discovered, all others in the dormitory have been moved to a more secure part of the prison. Brixton holds more than 1,000 prisoners, of whom more than three quarters are on remand, with many of the rest serving sentences of less than 18 months.

(*The Times*)

Prison cell forgery of cheque books

John Barclay, a prisoner in Maidstone jail, developed what his defence counsel described at Canterbury Crown Court yesterday as "a cottage industry devoted to the bespoke manufacture of cheque books and cheque cards".

Mr Barclay, aged 35, Gordon Lewis, aged 33, of Aylesford, Kent, and Brian Marshall, aged 38, of Chelsea, all admitted conspiracy to defraud.

Mr Marshall also admitted stealing a cheque book, a driving licence and health insurance cards, and Mr Lewis admitted dishonestly handling them.

They were bound over for three years to come up for judgement if called on by the court. Mr Lewis and Mr Marshall were each ordered to pay £100 towards the prosecution costs.

Mr Terry Boston, for the prosecution, said a routine search uncovered photographic copies of cheque cards in Mr Barclay's cell. Police officers later took away a printing outfit which he used to make cheque books. Mr Lewis, who visited Mr Barclay, suggested he could print the books on his equipment.

Mr Barclay told the police that he agreed to make the forgeries in return for new clothes when released. The still unused forgeries were found in Mr Marshall's possession.

The police have found that the printing set was posted to Mr Barclay at Maidstone prison, but do not know who sent it or why Mr Barclay was allowed to have it.

(*The Times*)

Fag end of the evening

From UPI in Dallas

A 35-year-old woman who was awakened by an unknown man crawling into her bed marched him out at gunpoint, only to have him knock on her door a few moments later and ask for a light for his cigarette.

The woman told police she awoke to find a partially clad man crawling into her bed whispering: "I want you, I love you." She responded by grabbing a small pistol from her nightstand and telling him: "I'll kill you. I want you out of my house."

The woman said she forced the man out of her apartment at gunpoint, locked the door, and called the police. But within seconds, there was a knock on the door. She opened it, its chain still in place, to find her assailant calmly asking her for a light for his cigarette. The astounded woman said she got her lighter, complied with his request, and re-locked the door.

Police arrived to see the man running from the woman's porch carrying a lighted cigarette, and arrested a 20-year-old suspect a short time later.

(*The Guardian*)

Stories

A A dream

1 Use the words in the box to complete the text.

> already   back   before   by myself   camped
> campsites   convenient   deep   dishes   drive
> facilities   fast   got   in time   metres
> moonlight   near   noise   outside   parked
> pitched   place   pleasant   puzzled   realised
> shining   sleeping bag   started   stream   supper
> tell   there   threw   touching   trouble
> twice   undressed   went to sleep   without
> woken   wood

A few years ago, I went on a camping holiday in the Pyrenees, in the south of France, in late September. I sometimes ....1.... in public ....2.... – they are mostly clean and well run, and it's ....3.... to have toilets, showers and so on. But more often I camped rough. I didn't mind not having the ....4...., and it was ....5.... to be ....6.....

One evening I found a wonderful ....7.... to camp, quite high up in the mountains. I ....8.... my car down a track, a hundred ....9.... or so away from the road, and ....10.... my tent in a small ....11.... by a ....12..... I made ....13...., washed the ....14.... in the stream, and went out for a walk in the ....15..... Then I ....16...., ...17.... into my ....18...., took a last look at the moon and ....19.....

I was ....20.... in the middle of the night by a rustling ....21..... At first I thought ....22.... was an animal moving around ....23..... Then I thought perhaps it was branches ....24.... the tent – but there weren't any trees ....25.... enough. I looked out of the tent, and for a moment I was ....26..... Everything looked completely different – white and ....27...., and strangely flat in the moonlight. Suddenly I ....28.... – snow! It was already quite ....29...., and coming down fast.

It looked very beautiful, but I was in ....30..... If I didn't move ....31.... I might not get away ....32.... the snow blocked the roads – indeed, it might ....33.... be too late to get the car ....34.... to the road. ....35.... waiting to dress, I took down the tent as fast as I could, ...36.... everything into the car and ....37.... driving. It was hard to ....38.... where the track was, and ....39.... I got stuck. But at last I managed to get to the road and ....40.... down the mountain out of the snowstorm – just ....41......

2 Vocabulary revision. Do you know the names for all these different kinds of container? See how many you can write *before* you look at the words below.

> bag   basin   basket   bin   bottle
> box   briefcase   cup   cupboard
> drawer   jug   mug   filing cabinet
> pot   saucepan   suitcase   teapot
> tin (can)

3 Grammar revision. Look at these regular verbs with their past tenses. What kind of words have a double letter in the past?

stop – stopped	wait – waited
seem – seemed	start – started
pin – pinned	rub – rubbed
end – ended	fit – fitted
hope – hoped	hop – hopped

Now write the past tenses of these verbs.

slip   aim   jam   knit   fail
clean   slim   fire   spot   grin

4 Grammar revision. Make questions.

1. My mother lived in Scotland when she was a girl. (*enjoy?*)

   Did she enjoy living in Scotland?

2. My father worked in a bank until he retired. (*like?*)
3. Our house was burgled last night. (*anything valuable?*)
4. Mike Gabb has just been killed in a plane crash. (*know well?*)
5. I went to university in Ireland. (*what study?*)
6. We all went to the opera last Saturday. (*children enjoy?*)
7. Katy has just bought herself a red leather jacket. (*how much cost?*)

5 Read these texts with a dictionary.

DREAMING
Cold-blooded animals such as reptiles and fish do not dream, but warm-blooded ones, including mammals and birds, do. By studying rapid eye movements (REMs) during sleep – which in humans is a sure sign of dreaming – French physiologist Michel Jouvet found that animals invariably dream more when they are younger. Animals like calves and foals, which can fend for themselves immediately after birth, dream more in the womb and less after being born than do animals like kittens and human babies, which are dependent on parental care.

A DREAM
Elias Howe spent years trying to perfect a sewing machine. One night he dreamed that he had been captured by a primitive tribe and was sentenced to be speared to death if he didn't produce a sewing machine within twenty-four hours. Howe racked his brains for the right solution, but in vain. When the deadline was up, the warriors surrounded Howe and raised their spears to kill him. Suddenly Howe woke up, leaped out of bed, and rushed to his laboratory. He had noticed that each spear had an eye-shaped hole near its point and his problem was solved. To make a sewing machine that worked, the hole had to be at the tip of the needle, not at the top or middle.

(from *Curious Facts* by John May)

6 Write about a personal experience using one of these beginnings.

1. Several years ago my friends/family and I decided to go on a camping/walking/touring holiday in . . .
2. I do not usually believe in the supernatural, but once I experienced something very strange indeed. I was . . .

Unit 6

B My heart is too full for words

1 Grammar revision: reported speech. What did they say?

SHE: Have you seen the new film at the Odeon?

She asked him if he'd seen the new film at the Odeon.

HE: It's terrible.

He said it was terrible.

SHE: What's so bad about it?
HE: My five-year-old daughter can write better dialogue.
SHE: Is there anything else on that you're interested in?
HE: There's the new Jarman film at the Regent.
SHE: What time is it on?
HE: Seven-fifteen; do you want to go?
SHE: How long does it last?
HE: It's over at half past nine. We'll make it if we hurry.
SHE: Have we got to take a bus?
HE: No, we can walk.
SHE: OK, I've heard it's good. I can't stay out too late though.
HE: You're walking a bit fast for me.
SHE: Sorry. It's my job that makes me do that.
HE: Are you going to get that promotion you put in for?
SHE: I don't know yet.

2 Put in *say, says, said, saying, tell, tells, told* or *telling*. If you have trouble, you can consult the rule on page 137.

1. 'Where's Alan? He .... he'd be here at six.'
2. 'Did he? He .... me he'd be here at half past.'
3. 'Typical. He never .... the same thing twice.'
4. 'The other day he .... to Debbie that he was moving to London.'
5. 'And then he .... John he'd got a job in New York.'
6. 'Working in a news agency, he .... me.'
7. 'Jane .... he .... her he was going to Australia.'
8. 'Do you know what he .... to me last week?'
9. 'No, I can't imagine. Do .... me.'
10. 'He only .... me his uncle had died and left him three million dollars.'
11. 'That would be nice. He .... he was going to marry me.'
12. 'Well, I'll .... one thing for him – he keeps you interested. So where is he?'
13. 'I'd .... he's either in Australia, or on a plane to New York, or still in bed, or .... somebody else he's going to marry her.'

"I thought I might stay in tonight and read my jacket."

3 In this dialogue, B is a rich banker who has been kidnapped by T, a mad terrorist. B is afraid of being killed, and agrees with everything T says. Write B's answers.

T: I don't like spinach.
B: *Nor do I.*
T: I like cauliflower, though.
B: *So do I.*
T: I can't stand people who wear rings on their little fingers.
B: ....1...........
T: I had a cousin who wore a ring on her little finger.
B: ....2...........
T: I've got a lot of admiration for rattlesnakes.
B: ....3...........
T: I haven't got any idea why people think rattlesnakes are ugly.
B: ....4...........
T: I can understand being a little scared of them, though.
B: ....5...........
T: I'm not scared of them, though.
B: ....6...........
T: When I was younger I didn't like school.
B: ....7...........
T: I'm not in favour of making kids go to school.
B: ....8...........
T: I wouldn't make one of my kids go to school.
B: ....9...........
T: I think schools are at the bottom of everything that's wrong with our society.
B: ....10...........

4 Write these fractions in words and say them aloud. Be careful to pronounce *th* correctly.

1/9   one ninth
3/10   three tenths

1/7	1/11	1/10	1/8	3/7
4/11	7/10	5/8	9/13	11/24
6/15	2/5			

5 Read the letter, using a dictionary if necessary.

```
                                    17 Harlow Road
                                    East Muirhead
                                    Edinburgh EH6 7BK

                                    18th June, 1987


Dear Alice,

Thanks a lot for your letter. It was good to hear from
you and to get all your news. I was sorry to hear about
Jeremy, but at least I'm glad the kids are doing so
well.

I was interested to hear about your plan for a book
about people's earliest memories. You're certainly
welcome to mine - I hope you can use it.

I must have been about two at the time - certainly no
older than two and a half, because we still lived by
the sea. I was playing by the big window in our front
room, where I used to sit on wet days looking at the
rain on the window and listening to the sea crashing on
the beach. That window was very important to me - I can
remember not only the way it looked, but also the feel
of the window-pane against my face, and even the taste
of the glass - you know how children like to touch
everything with their mouths. Well, while I was playing
I heard a noise outside in the street - people
shouting, something like that. So I ran over to the
window and looked out. And there was a fight going on
in the street. Two men were hitting each other, and a
lot of women and children were watching them and
shouting. Then one of the men fell over and the other
man ran away. It looked a bit like my Daddy, but I
wasn't sure. I don't know whether I asked him
afterwards or not. I felt strange about it. I was
neither frightened not excited, but it must have
affected me quite deeply, because I still remember it
very vividly, as if it had happened yesterday. And I
have very few other memories from that time. Even now,
if I see the sea through a window it reminds me of that
strange fight.

Love to Andy and Phil. And good luck with the book.

Love,
```

Eve

6 Write a letter, using the following 'skeleton' as a basis. Invent an English-speaking friend to write to if you don't have a real one. You can change the order of words, and make any other changes you need to, but you must use plenty of the words and expressions in the skeleton.

ADDRESS
DATE

Dear ....

Thanks a lot for your letter. It was good to hear from you and to get all your news. I was sorry to hear about ...., but at least I'm glad ....

I was interested to hear about your plan for a book about people's earliest memories. You're certainly welcome to mine – I hope you can use it.

I must have been .... at the time – certainly no older than ...., because ....
I was ....ing ...., where .... That .... was very important to me – I can remember not only ...., but also ....
Well, while I was ....ing I .... a ....
So I .... and ....
And there was a ....
Then .... and ....
I was neither .... nor ...., but it must have affected me quite deeply, because I still remember it very vividly, as if it had happened yesterday. Even now, if I see ...., it reminds me of ....

Love to .... and .... And good luck with the book.

Love,

YOUR NAME

7 Read the text and answer the questions.

The cell door slammed behind Rubashov.

He remained leaning against the door for a few seconds, and lit a cigarette. On the bed to his right lay two fairly clean blankets, and the straw mattress looked newly filled. The washbasin to his left had no plug, but the tap functioned. The pail next to it had been freshly disinfected, it did not smell. The walls on both sides were of solid brick, which would stifle the sound of tapping, but where the heating and drain pipe penetrated it, it had been plastered and resounded quite well; besides, the heating pipe itself seemed to be noise-conducting. The window started at eye-level; one could see down into the courtyard without having to pull oneself up by the bars. So far everything was in order.

He yawned, took his coat off, rolled it up and put it on the mattress as a pillow. He looked out into the yard. The snow shimmered yellow in the double light of the moon and the electric lamps. All round the yard, along the walls, a narrow track had been cleared for the daily exercise. Dawn had not yet appeared; the stars still shone clear and frostily, in spite of the lamps. On the rampart of the outside wall, which lay opposite Rubashov's cell, a soldier with his rifle at the slope was marching the hundred paces up and down; he stamped at every step as if on parade. From time to time the yellow light of the lamps flashed on his bayonet.

Rubashov took his shoes off, still standing at the window. He put out his cigarette, laid the stub on the floor at the end of his bedstead, and remained sitting on the mattress for a few minutes. He went back to the window once more. The courtyard was still; the sentry was just turning; above the machine-gun tower he saw a streak of the Milky Way.

Rubashov stretched himself on the bunk and wrapped himself in the top blanket. It was five o'clock and it was unlikely that one had to get up here before seven in winter. He was very sleepy and, thinking it over, decided that he would hardly be brought up for examination for another three or four days. He took his pince-nez off, laid them on the stone-paved floor next to the cigarette stub, smiled and shut his eyes. He was warmly wrapped up in the blanket, and felt protected; for the first time in months he was not afraid of his dreams.

When a few minutes later the warder turned the light off from outside, and looked through the spy-hole into his cell, Rubashov, ex-Commissar of the People, slept, his back turned to the wall, with his head on his outstretched left arm, which stuck stiffly out of the bed; only the hand on the end of it hung loosely and twitched in his sleep.

(from *Darkness at Noon* by Arthur Koestler – adapted)

1. Do you think Rubashov has been in prison before? Give reasons for your answer.
2. Why do you think the 'sound of tapping' is mentioned?
3. What do you think the 'daily exercise' consists of?
4. What do you think Rubashov has been dreaming about for the past few months?
5. What country do you think the story takes place in?

Travel

A The sun was in the north

1 Grammar revision. Can you put in the right prepositions?

1. The Phoenicians travelled right round Africa .... small boats.
2. The journey was planned .... Necho .... 600 BC.
3. He was interested .... finding a sea route .... the Red Sea .... the Mediterranean.
4. .... those days, nobody knew how big Africa was.
5. The Phoenicians lived .... the eastern end .... the Mediterranean.
6. They set off .... the beginning of winter.
7. Month .... month went by; they were amazed to see that the sun was now .... the north .... midday.
8. .... six months the coast turned west.
9. While they were sailing .... the west coast of Africa they ran out .... food.
10. It took eighteen months .... them to reach Morocco.
11. They had been away .... over two years.
12. Nicolo and Maffeo Polo stayed in China .... a long time.
13. Marco kept a diary .... his experiences.
14. They landed .... the Turkish coast.
15. They rode .... Iran, Afghanistan and Mongolia.
16. Marco's illness delayed them .... a year.
17. .... the way they saw wonderful things which were unknown .... Europe.
18. They saw a liquid that came .... the ground and could be used .... fuel.
19. .... 1275 they arrived .... China.
20. Marco was amazed to find a country that was far more civilised .... Italy.
21. .... his diary he described cities .... Hangzhou.
22. There were bridges high enough .... ships to go ....
23. The emperor took a special interest .... Marco.
24. When they arrived back .... Italy, they told their friends .... their experiences.
25. Nobody would believe their stories .... the strange countries .... the east.

"Hello, folks, this is your Captain speaking. May I introduce my best friend, Boko? Boko flies the aeroplane when I'm not feeling well."

2 Grammar revision. Simple past or past progressive?

1. I (*mend*) my sails one day when a man I had worked with before (*walk*) up and (*ask*) me if I'd like to have a drink.
2. I (*think*) he probably had more than just a friendly drink in mind, so I (*stop*) what I (*do*), (*wipe*) off my hands, and (*follow*) him to the local drink shop.
3. It (*be*) there that I (*find*) out that he (*recruit*) people to work on Necho's project.
4. Nowadays, everybody knows about our journey, but then, it (*sound*) a bit strange.
5. At first I thought the man (*try*) to play a trick on me.
6. But the more he (*talk*), the better it (*sound*) – a real adventure.
7. I (*get*) tired of the same old sea routes year after year.
8. Besides, I (*think*) it would be a great trading opportunity; the route to Carthage, across Greek waters, (*get*) more and more dangerous.
9. You may not believe this, but it (*only take*) me a few minutes to decide; I (*sit*) there in that shop with a cup in my hand, and I (*make*) a decision that would change my life – and lots of other people's lives as well.
10. There were times on the journey when I (*have*) doubts about my decision.
11. Once while we (*be*) pushed south-west by the monsoon winds, I (*nearly be*) washed off the deck by a big wave.
12. And one day during the long sail south, one of the men (*try*) to convince the rest of us that we were under a magic spell when a dead black bird (*fall*) on the deck; believe me, we (*be*) scared.
13. But there were some good times, too: we (*have*) to stop and collect supplies on the west coast, and we (*stay*) there for a long time, in one of the most beautiful places I've seen.
14. One evening while I (*sit*) under a tree with the wind in my face and a luscious big mango to eat, I almost (*decide*) to stay there for the rest of my life.
15. But of course I (*not stay*); I (*know*) that I would get tired of it soon enough, and besides, my wife and children (*wait*) for me back in Tyre.
16. We (*see*) thousands of birds at Gibraltar, but these (*be*) alive: they (*fly*) over, on their way south for the winter.
17. In December, when I (*get*) home, I (*make*) sure that no one told my family before I (*arrive*).
18. When I (*walk*) through the door, my wife (*put*) supper on the table, and my son and daughter – whom I (*hardly recognise*) – (*play*) by the fireplace.
19. I (*know*) when I (*see*) them that I had done the right thing not to stay under that tree.
20. I still think of that big tree in the jungle sometimes, though; and I'll bet there's not a man who (*go*) on that journey who wouldn't like to go back.

3 Guessing unknown words. Read the text, and then try and find words to match the definitions below.

First paragraph:
1. stay
2. a sheet of printed paper, usually given free to the public

Second paragraph:
3. The government body that can give a plane the right to fly
4. ways of getting out of somewhere
5. reason for doing something

Third paragraph:
6. a material that has air bubbles in it

Fourth paragraph:
7. things you have bought
8. small place for storing things, with a door or lid
9. making

Sixth paragraph:
10. found
11. stopped (used about fires)
12. people getting out of a place

THIS IS YOUR CAPTAIN SPEAKING

'Ladies and gentlemen, this is your captain speaking. I regret to tell you that the aircraft is on fire, and we are about to make an emergency landing. Now there is absolutely nothing to worry about. I would like you all to remain seated, with your seatbelts fastened, until the aircraft comes to a complete stop, and then leave via the emergency exits. If you haven't already read the leaflet in the seat pocket in front of you, I suggest now would be a good time. Oh, and by the way, you should have ninety seconds to get out.

'Look, I know there are 450 of you back there, and ninety seconds may not seem too long, but it can be done. If it makes you feel any better, I can tell you that when this plane was built they got 450 people out of the factory and sat them down where you're sitting, and then shouted "fire". *They* all got out within ninety seconds, otherwise the FAA would never have given this thing a licence. Okay, so there wasn't any real fire, and maybe they could use all the exits, but they didn't have your motivation, now did they?

'I suppose some of you must be wondering what happens if you don't make it in ninety seconds. Yes, well, I'm glad you asked that question. You may have noticed that there is quite a lot of plastic in this aeroplane, and your seats are filled with polyurethane foam. Now it doesn't burn very easily, but I have to tell you that when it does catch fire it gives off rather a lot of smoke and a few gases. Carbon monoxide, hydrogen cyanide; stuff like that. It does get a bit hot, too. About 1000 degrees Centigrade after two minutes, if you really want to know. So if I were you I'd try to make it in ninety seconds.

'Just a couple of other things you ought to know. About your duty-free purchases: I expect most of you have got bottles of whisky and brandy in the overhead lockers and we'll just have to hope those bottles don't break, won't we, because boy does that stuff burn! And then there are your clothes. I noticed most of you were wearing some when you came on board, which is a bit of a pity, really. There's nothing like a good woollen suit for generating hydrogen cyanide when the fire really gets going.

'Now, if you sit tight I'm going to try to get this thing on the ground without breaking anything. And, er, in case I don't get another opportunity, thank you for flying with ____ Airlines.'

Fictional, of course, but those are the odds which face a passenger unlucky enough to be caught in an in-flight fire. Time is the vital factor. If the fire cannot be traced and extinguished by the crew, and fairly quickly at that, the aircraft has to be landed as rapidly as possible. Once on the ground, hopefully intact, evacuation must be immediate and swift before smoke and gas snuff out the lives of all on board. Many have died because they did not get to the emergency exits in time.

(from *The Unsafe Sky* by William Norris)

4 Copy the words and underline the stressed syllable in each word. Use your dictionary if necessary. Practise saying the words with the correct stress.

arrive   avoid   become
begin   believe   businessman
civilised   control   delay
difficult   discover
enormous   experience
fantastic   interested
journey   Portuguese
publish   report   travel
unknown   welcome
wonderful

5 Read the letter. Then write another letter of complaint to a tour operator constructed in the same way. You can base your letter on the notes, or imagine your own situation.

Notes:
- rented cottage for one week, May 7–14 (£125)
- 'The Yews' near Lake Windermere
- Lakeland Leisure Ltd, P.O. Box 32, Kendal, Cumbria
- advertisement: 'charming cottage, newly furnished and carpeted throughout'
- arrival. damp and mould (downstairs very bad); dirty; vacuum cleaner didn't work; overflowing dustbins
- no other accommodation available, so stayed
- 15 May: wrote asking for compensation for poor state of cottage and loss of enjoyment
- 22 May: still no reply

19 Coniston Way
Hemel Hempstead
Herts WD4 8MY

Sunway Tours Ltd   15 October 1987
33 Brooklands Avenue
Watford
Herts WD1 2NP

Dear Sir or Madam,

In April I booked a villa party holiday in the Algarve with your company for October 3-10. I paid £250 for the holiday, including breakfast and dinner provided by a cook plus £21 for a single room supplement. *booking details*

Two days before my departure, someone from your office phoned me to say that the villa was overbooked, and to ask if I would accept a 4-star hotel instead. I replied that I would rather not go abroad. I was reassured later that same day (October 1) that my original booking still stood. On my arrival at the airport your representative said that there was no problem. *what happened*

On arriving at the villa however, I found that it had been fully booked by a family group and that I had been moved into a nearby bungalow without being asked. I was given meal vouchers for meals at a nearby hotel, but these did not cover the full costs of meals. *the problem*

You advertised, and I paid for, a specific type of holiday. *summarise* This type of holiday was not available, and I was forced under protest to accept inferior accommodation. I have booked with your company twice before and have always been very happy with my holidays; I am very surprised that this has happened. *say the company is good* I am sure you will agree that it is only fair that I be offered compensation for my inconvenience. Could you please let me know as soon as possible what compensation you plan to give me? *demand compensation politely*

I look forward to hearing from you soon.

Yours faithfully,

Sandra Banarjee

Sandra Banarjee (Ms)

Unit 7

B You can say that again

1 Vocabulary revision. The following words and expressions are all connected with travel. Can you divide them into three groups, under the headings 'road', 'rail' and 'air'? Some of them will go in more than one group.

boarding pass	change	check-in	check the oil
compartment	crossroads	delay	driver
emergency exit	flight	map	motorway
no smoking	petrol station	pilot	platform
return ticket	roadworks	seatbelt	
security check	speed limit	stewardess	
ticket collector			

ROAD	RAIL	AIR
check the oil	compartment	boarding pass

2 Revision. Put in the right prepositions.

A: How long have you been waiting in this queue?
B: ....1.... ten o'clock. How about you?
A: ....2.... about 45 minutes.
C: Next please. May I see your papers? Thank you. Oh dear. You haven't got your birth certificate. You'll have to come back. Can you be here ....3.... 3.45 pm ....4.... Monday?
B: That's very difficult. I work ....5.... the afternoon. Could we possibly make it one morning?
C: How about 10.15 ....6.... Tuesday?
B: I can't manage Tuesday. Suppose I could get my birth certificate to you before you close this morning? When do you close?
C: We'll be closing for lunch ....7.... about 45 minutes. But we're open this afternoon ....8.... 2.00 ....9.... 5.30.
B: I'll try to get back ....10.... one.
C: Fine, just come straight up to this window.
B: Thank you.
C: Not at all. Next please.
A: I've come to get a certificate for my mother. I think her records are here.
C: When was she born?
A: ....11.... 1916. August 16th.
C: Oh, that's all right then. You see, we have the files up to 1950, but all of the files ....12.... 1950 have been computerised.
A: That's a relief. I've got off work specially to come down and sort this out.
C: Just fill in this form and I'll have your certificate ready ....13.... about fifteen minutes.
A: Thank you very much.

3 Grammar revision. Write the 'short answers'.

1. 'Are you staying long?'
   'No, I'm not.'
2. 'You can get cheap flights, can't you?'
   'Yes, I can.'
3. 'You've lost the key, have you?' 'Yes, ...'
4. 'Tiring flight, isn't it?' 'Yes, ...'
5. 'Are you George Temple?' 'No, ...'
6. 'Do you fly a lot?' 'No, ...'
7. 'Drive carefully, won't you?' 'Yes, ...'
8. 'You must get ready to leave.' 'Yes, I suppose ....'
9. 'Did you know Peter Lewis?' 'No, I'm afraid ....'
10. 'It should be a quick flight.' 'Yes, I think ....'
11. 'Is there a customs check at the border?' 'Yes, ...'

4 Grammar revision. Write the 'reply questions'.

1. 'I work for BCJ Electrical Components.'
   'Oh, do you?'
2. 'He's the Deputy Sales Manager.'
   'Is he really?'
3. 'I'm off to Canada tomorrow.'
   'Oh, ...?'
4. 'She runs five miles a day.'
   '............ really?'
5. 'The Slaters have just got divorced.' 'Oh, ...?'
6. 'It's snowing.' 'Oh, ...?'
7. 'It's getting late. I must go now.' 'Oh, ... really?'

"Now if the passengers on the left hand side will put their left arms through the windows and do this – while those on the right hand side…"

5 Grammar revision. Write the 'question tags'.

1. It's cold, *isn't it?*
2. You're not ready, *are you?*
3. You speak Greek, ...?
4. She can't swim, ...?
5. They're late, ...?
6. The new car looks good, ...?
7. You can drive, ...?
8. Henry wasn't there yesterday, ...?
9. The grass needs cutting, ...?
10. She doesn't look at all like her sister, ...?
11. You won't tell anybody, ...?
12. Your mother lived in Japan when she was younger, ...?

6 Read one or more of these. You can use your dictionary.

Pilot holds New York hostage

'This is the first airplane hostage situation in the history of the world with New York City as the hostage.'

That was how the police department described yesterday's bizarre incident in which a dissatisfied Australian writer threatened to crash his aircraft into a New York skyscraper.

The first word of the threat came at 10.20am when a police department official telephoned the United Nations and informed the Secretary General that a lunatic pilot in the area planned to fly his plane into the UN building.

The UN was evacuated, bomb disposal squads and fire teams moved onto the UN grounds to cope with the threatened disaster. Traffic outside the UN was re-routed and no one was allowed on First Avenue but reporters.

Then the police corrected their original report. The target of the pilot, Richard Boudin, was not the UN, but the publishing company of Harcourt Brace Jovanovich, housed in a building two blocks from the UN.

Mr Boudin apparently felt that his novel, *Confessions of a Promiscuous Counterfeiter*, was not getting enough publicity, so he chartered the plane at a New Jersey airport and radioed that he was going to destroy the publishing house.

Soon after noon the president of the publishing company agreed to talk with Mr Boudin, if he would land at La Guardia Airport. Mr Boudin accepted and flew off, the crisis over.

Police said Mr Boudin would be charged with reckless endangerment and other offences.

(from an article by Jane Rosen in *The Guardian* – adapted)

Chipmunk lands in Heathrow darkness

Officials are to investigate how a light aircraft landed undetected on an unlit runway at Heathrow Airport in London.

The single engine de Havilland Chipmunk was found by a routine British Airports Authority patrol on the grass a few yards from one of Heathrow's two main runways. The runway was closed at the time.

Customs officials with dogs searched the aircraft, but police said there was no suggestion at the moment that it had been used for smuggling, or terrorist activities.

But how did the plane land unnoticed at the world's busiest airport? A spokeswoman for the Civil Aviation Authority, which is responsible for air traffic control, guessed that it must have touched down while there was 'no known traffic' – no scheduled flights taking off or landing – on the other, open runway. So radar monitoring was unnecessary.

The authorities at Heathrow automatically prepared an invoice of landing and parking charges incurred by the Chipmunk. It came to just under £37.

But the CAA's spokeswoman said: 'Until the whole matter is resolved, we don't know whether the invoice will be sent to anyone, or, if it is, to whom.'

(from an article by John Hooper in *The Guardian* – adapted)

The train not stopping at platform one...

British Rail passengers from London to Oxford had an unscheduled detour via Swindon after a train driver forgot to stop at Didcot.

People getting ready to change for a connecting train to Oxford on Saturday evening heard the guard announce Didcot on the train intercom, only to see the station flash past them.

The 30 Oxford-bound passengers eventually reached journey's end 45 minutes late, after getting a train back from Swindon to Didcot to catch another local train home.

Mrs Jean Robinson, an Oxford health expert who was one of the passengers affected, said they had been offered no explanation or apology for what happened.

'It was fortunate the train was one that stopped at Swindon; otherwise we'd have gone to Bristol,' she said.

'When we got out at Swindon there was no one to tell us anything and we couldn't find anyone in charge.'

A British Rail spokesman said this week that the driver had simply forgotten to stop at Didcot. 'It's an error which is regretted,' he said.

(from an article in *The Oxford Times* – adapted)

7 Choose one of the following. Use words and expressions from Unit 7 of the Student's Book in your writing.

1. Imagine that an old man is coming to visit you. He is travelling by air, and has never flown before. Write a letter telling him what to expect and giving him some advice.
2. Write the story of a difficult or dangerous journey that you have made.

"I hope it comes soon – this cartoon is supposed to be about travel."

Unit 8

Believing and imagining

A Evidence

1 Grammar revision: irregular verbs. Write the infinitive, past and participle of each verb.

INFINITIVE	PAST	PARTICIPLE
awake	awoke	awoken
become	....	....
....	began	....
....	....	broken
bring	....	....
....	burnt	....
....	....	come
drive	....	....
....	ate	....
....	....	found
fly	....	....
....	went	....
....	....	kept
know	....	....
....	left	....
....	....	made
ride	....	....
....	ran	....
....	....	said
see	....	....
....	....	taken
tell	....	....

2 Complex sentences. Use the structure *Are you sure (that) it is/was...?* to write replies to the sentences, as in the examples.

1. The tooth fairy puts the money there. (*tooth fairy*)

   Are you sure it's the tooth fairy that puts the money there?

2. John was looking for a bungalow near London. (*bungalow*)

   Are you sure it was a bungalow that John was looking for?

3. The telephone's ringing. (*telephone*)
4. They speak French in Mali. (*French*)
5. I need another drink. (*another drink*)
6. We decided on Tuesday for the meeting. (*Tuesday*)
7. My husband sent me these flowers for my birthday. (*your husband*)
8. I'm feeling ill – those shrimps have upset me. (*the shrimps*)
9. That girl keeps looking at me. (*you*)
10. Carol's madly in love with Simon. (*Simon*)

"I don't care what planet you're from, you can't run around earth stark naked!"

3 Use one of the structures in the box to introduce the sentences, as in the examples.

It seems/seemed obvious that . . . (not) . . .
It seems/seemed (un)likely that . . .
It seems/seemed possible that . . .
It looks/looked as if . . .
It doesn't/didn't look as if . . .
It sounds/sounded as if . . .
It doesn't/didn't sound as if . . .
I wonder/wondered whether . . .

1. We are alone in the universe.
   It seems unlikely that we are alone in the universe.
2. There are living creatures on other planets.
   It seems obvious that there are living creatures on other planets.
3. There are people like us on Mars.
4. We will make contact with creatures from other worlds in the next twenty years.
5. They will be very like us.
6. We will get on well together.
7. The weather was going to get worse.
8. It was going to snow.
9. We would have trouble getting home.
10. The road over the mountains was open.
11. The thunder was right over our heads.
12. We would be struck by lightning.

4 Complete the text with words from the box.

according   at all   believes   Christmas
dinosaurs   evidence   horoscope
impression   it's   mind   moon   needs
noises   obvious   one   prove   reason
religions   saving   sounds   wrong

Julie is the kind of person who ....1.... in anything. Anything ....2..... She believes in reincarnation, telepathy, witches, black magic, white magic, and all of the world's ....3.... at the same time. She doesn't need ....4.... for her beliefs – it's just ....5.... to her that they're true. I sometimes have the ....6.... that Julie still believes in Father ....7.... – and she's 34 years old. For some ....8.... or other, she just ....9.... to believe in the supernatural.

Julie lives in an old house in the country. I go and stay with her sometimes, and I must say I have trouble getting to sleep because of all the ....10.... that you get in an old house. It ....11.... to me as if there's something ....12.... with the central heating, but that doesn't satisfy Julie. She's sure that ....13.... ghosts that make the noises, and she walks round the house for hours at night hoping to see ....14.....

Julie is ....15.... up money to go to Egypt and study the pyramids. ....16.... to her, it's obvious that they were built by refugees from the ....17...., and she's planning to write a book to ....18.... it. Either that, or she's going to organise an expedition to Central Africa to prove that ....19.... are still alive. She hasn't quite decided which yet, but she has an astrologer friend who is making a detailed ....20.... for her, and that should help her to make up her ....21.....

5 Write two or three paragraphs about one of the following subjects. Use some of the words and expressions from Exercise 4 of Student's Book Lesson 8A.

1. A person you know who doesn't believe in anything.
2. What did you believe in when you were a child?
3. Do you believe in ghosts or in life after death? Why (not)?
4. Do you believe that the earth has been visited by creatures from other parts of space? Why (not)?
5. Do you think it is ever possible for people to see into the future? Why (not)?

6 Read these texts, using a dictionary if necessary.

1. In May 1957 seven people were sitting in a dining room just after lunch. Suddenly a man in brown walked past the open door into the kitchen. Four of the people saw him, and one got up to ask him what he wanted. The man had vanished, yet he could not have left the house unseen. Only then did the people realise that they must have seen a ghost.

2. This happened near Sydney, Australia, one evening in 1873. Six weeks after Captain Towns died, his married daughter entered a bedroom where there was a burning gas lamp. Reflected in the shiny surface of the wardrobe was a 'portrait' of her father. His thin, pale face, and grey flannel jacket were unmistakable. A young lady with the daughter saw the image too. They called other members of the household. Altogether eight people came and marvelled at the apparition. But when the Captain's widow tried to touch it, the image faded away.

3. An old man was seen trudging home through a stormy night, dressed only in pyjamas. The driver who passed him on the road discovered that the old man had died three weeks before.

4. One night in 1976, a woman awoke to see a tall, thin female figure in her bedroom. The phantom pressed skinny fingers around the woman's throat as if to strangle her. Then the grip relaxed, and the figure faded. Later, the victim described the ghost to her fiancé. The description fitted his long-dead Malaysian grandmother.

"It's good for a man to have a hobby."

5. In 1964 a huge press was accidentally set moving inside a Detroit car factory. A nearby worker claimed his life was saved only by a tall, scarred black man who pushed him clear of the machinery. No one with him saw that person, but some recognised the description. It fitted a black worker accidentally killed there 20 years before.

6. In the middle 1800s, a young girl was walking down an English country lane. Suddenly she seemed to see her mother lying on a bedroom floor. The girl fetched a doctor and they found her mother exactly as the girl described her. The woman had fallen with a heart attack. Luckily the doctor arrived in time to save her life.

7. In 1926, two women on a country walk near Bury St Edmunds in Suffolk, England, saw a big house in a garden surrounded by a high wall. Soon afterwards they passed that way again. They found only overgrown waste land that had not been disturbed for years.

(from *Piccolo Explorer Book of Mysteries*)

Unit 8

B Secret thoughts

1 Vocabulary revision. What are these things made of? Can you write the names of all the materials? Use a dictionary if necessary.

2 Look at the pictures. How could you warn the people? Examples:

'Don't open the door, or you'll get wet.'
'Look out! If you open the door, you'll get wet.'

A   B   C   D   E   F

3 Grammar. Some verbs are not often used in progressive forms. Examples are *think* and *feel* (used to talk about people's opinions); *hope*; *want*; *know*; *believe*; *like*; *love*; *need*; *remember*; *understand*; *seem*; *look* (meaning *appear, seem*). Can you put in the correct verb forms?

1. 'Would you like to come out for a drink' 'Sorry, I (*work*).'
2. 'How do you like my hair?' 'I (*think*) it (*look*) great.'
3. 'Where's Deborah?' 'I (*believe*) she (*play*) tennis.'
4. 'George (*come*) next weekend, isn't he?' 'I'm not sure, but I (*hope*) so.'
5. 'There's somebody on the phone. He says he (*want*) to talk to you.' 'Who is it?' 'I (*not know*).'
6. 'Hello. What (*you do*) these days?' 'Sorry – I (*remember*) your face, but I'm afraid I've forgotten your name.'

4 Grammar. Put in the correct tenses.

I (*had / was having*) lunch in a small restaurant near the office. She (*sat / was sitting*) at a table near the window. I (*wondered / was wondering*) why she (*looked / was looking*) at me so intently. (*Did she know / Was she knowing*) me? I (*didn't think / wasn't thinking*) I (*ever saw / had ever seen*) her before. Suddenly she (*stood up / was standing up*) and (*walked / was walking*) slowly towards me. I (*still remember / am still remembering*) my feelings exactly. I (*wanted / was wanting*) to run away, but I (*knew / was knowing*) I couldn't. She (*stopped / was stopping*) by my table and (*smiled / was smiling*) down at me. She had on a purple dress – I (*think / 'm thinking*) it had a flower pattern – and she was amazingly beautiful. 'Excuse me,' she said. 'Have you got a light?'

5 Here is part of a political speech. Write the speaker's secret thoughts. (The first two are done for you.) Or if you prefer, write a new political speech with secret thoughts included.

My fellow Fantasians! (*1. You poor fools!*) This is a serious crisis in our country's affairs. (*2. In my affairs – if I don't get elected I'll have to find an honest job.*) If we are to come safely through the next five years, we must choose wisely. (*3.*) The Fantasian National Democratic Liberal Party is not interested in power for its own sake. (*4.*) It is interested in the welfare of the people. (*5.*) It is the party of the common man – and the common woman too. (*6.*) If you elect me, I will work day and night on your behalf. (*7.*) I will fight for better conditions for the workers. (*8.*) I will fight for higher wages. (*9.*) I will fight for better housing. (*10.*) Together, we will march towards a bright and glorious future. (*11.*) A future in which the citizens of this great country can join hands in peace and love. (*12.*) A future in which our children, and their children, will be proud to be Fantasians. (*13.*) Vote for me – for the FNDLP – for peace, democracy and freedom. (*14.*)

6 How imaginative are you? Answer the questions and check your score.

1. If you were expecting a friend to come round to your place and he/she was late, would you:
   a. assume something ordinary had happened to delay him/her, and not worry?
   b. feel slightly worried?
   c. think he/she must have been in an accident?

2. When other people tell you about their troubles, do you:
   a. feel very upset?
   b. feel bored?
   c. feel some sympathy?

3. When you look at clouds, do you:
   a. see pictures in them?
   b. feel thoughtful?
   c. think about the weather?

4. When you first meet somebody who attracts you, do you:
   a. think sensibly about your chances?
   b. think he/she is the most wonderful person in the world, and imagine yourselves living together?
   c. tell yourself not to lose your head?

5. While staying in an old house, you are woken up by strange noises. Do you think of:
   a. water pipes?
   b. burglars?
   c. ghosts?

6. Do you get an idea that you think would make a good book, film, poem or song:
   a. never?
   b. often?
   c. sometimes?

7. Do you daydream:
   a. often when you should be thinking about other things?
   b. sometimes?
   c. hardly ever?

8. Can you imagine yourself doing something that would cause you to go to prison?
   a. not at all
   b. with difficulty
   c. easily

9. When you talk about something that has happened to you, do you:
   a give all the details?
   b. change things to make it more interesting?
   c. just give the main points?

10. Which of these kinds of book or magazine article do you like most?
    a. biography/history
    b. fiction (novels, stories etc.)
    c. practical (information about how to do things)

(See score table and comments after Exercise 7.)

"Come on, it's your move!"

7 Try the crossword.

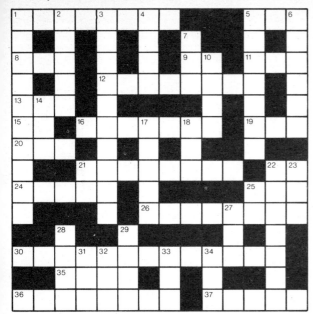

ACROSS

1. Animal that lived millions of years ago.
5. Not many.
8. A waiter will not call you this if you are a woman.
9. Preposition.
11. Move fast on foot.
12. Driver.
13. You've got one on each side of your nose.
15. Negative answer.
16. Military dress.
19. You've got one on each side of your head.
20. Past of *dig*.
21. An .... person does a lot of sport.
22. I'll ring you .... soon .... I arrive.
24. Loud unpleasant sound.
25. Solid water.
26. I don't think there's enough .... for the existence of ghosts.
30. If you park on a double yellow line, this person may give you a ticket (*two words*).
35. Post.
36. This probably won't stop you getting a parking ticket.
37. 'Have you ever seen a ....?' 'No, and anyway, I don't believe in them.'

DOWN

1. Some people think that birds are the ....s of the dinosaurs.
2. Person who looks after you in hospital.
3. I hope you don't meet this when you're swimming at the seaside.
4. Part of a textbook.
5. The opposite of *nearer*.
6. Walk about without any clear purpose.
7. .... example.
10. You see it in a cinema.
14. Not me. Not him. Not her. Not us. Not them.
17. Have you got .... teeth?
18. Unpopular animal.
21. The same as 22 across.
22. People from the north and south of the country speak with different ....
23. You do this with 13 across.
25. Not out.
27. 'I like a film to have a beginning, a middle and an ...., but not necessarily in that order.' (*Jean-Luc Godard*)
28. Mother.
29. You will find this in a filing cabinet.
31. If you get too ...., your clothes won't 32 down any more.
32. If your clothes don't ...., it may be because you're getting too 31 down.
33. Children's favourite question.
34. Small carpet.

(*Solution on page 137.*)

HOW IMAGINATIVE ARE YOU?

Your score:

1. a–1	b–2	c–3
2. a–3	b–1	c–2
3. a–3	b–2	c–1
4. a–2	b–3	c–1
5. a–1	b–2	c–3
6. a–1	b–3	c–2
7. a–3	b–2	c–1
8. a–1	b–2	c–3
9. a–2	b–3	c–1
10. a–2	b–3	c–1

TOTAL 10–16: You are a practical, down-to-earth person. You don't usually let your imagination run away with you, and you are not afraid of very much. But you may sometimes have trouble understanding other people's feelings.

TOTAL 17–23: You have an average amount of imagination, and you are quite good at understanding how other people feel. Sometimes you live too much inside your own head, but your common sense usually keeps you in touch with reality.

TOTAL 24–30: Your imagination is your greatest strength and your greatest weakness. On the one hand, you live a rich interior life, and you experience the pleasures and excitement of the true creative artist. However, you often suffer from irrational fears and superstitious beliefs. And you must be careful not to spend so much time watching the 'cinema' inside your own head that you completely lose touch with the real world.

Music

A I slid into it

1 Relative clauses. Join these sentences together with *which*. Use commas (,,) before and after the relative clause.

1. My house needs a lot doing to it. It is about 40 years old.

   My house, which needs a lot doing to it, is about 40 years old.

2. His violin is worth over £20,000. It once belonged to Beethoven.
3. Yesterday's meeting lasted six hours. It was a complete waste of time.
4. The average weekly wage used to be about £6. It is now about £185.
5. Penguins are completely unable to fly. They have no natural enemies.
6. This car keeps breaking down. I bought it from an ex-friend of mine.

   This car, which I bought from an ex-friend of mine, keeps breaking down.

7. My novel is going to be published next autumn. You didn't like it at all.
8. These glasses give me a headache. I have to wear them for reading.
9. Your letter took nine days to get here. You posted it on the seventeenth.
10. Folk music has gone out of fashion. I like it enormously.

2 Relative clauses. Make sentences using *which/that*. Don't use commas. (Why not?) Example:

Animals that eat meat are called 'carnivores'.

Animals	is on the table	are called	down.
The book	run on electricity	has all	the cat.
The snow	runs our heating	is for	melted.
Water	fell last night	is called	motors.
The pump	falls from the sky	has broken	'carnivores'.
The letter	is in that saucer	wasn't for	rain.
Engines	eat meat	are called	Helen.
The milk	came this morning	is for	me.

3 Relative clauses. Make sentences as in the example. Don't use *it* or *them*. Example:

I've lost the book Alice lent me.

BEGINNINGS	ENDS
I've lost the book	she had it last year
That's the same coat	Mary gave it to him
What's that picture	Alice lent it to me
Where are the papers	my doctor told me to take them
These are the pills	you're looking at it
He's wearing the ring	I put them on the table

"He's got no sense of rhythm."

HEATH

4 Conditionals. Imagine you have won a lot of money in a lottery. Here are the beginnings and ends of some sentences about the different things you can do with the money. Put the beginnings and ends together to make sensible sentences.

BEGINNINGS	ENDS
If I bet it all on a horse race	I'll almost certainly lose it.
If I spend it all on clothes	it'll certainly be safe.
If I give it all away	I might be sorry afterwards.
If I buy a house with it	I may not make very much income from it.
If I put it in the bank	I know I'll feel wonderful.

Now complete some of these sentences. Use the structures in the box to help you.

> I'll . . .
> I won't . . .
> I may/might (not) . . .
> I'll certainly/probably . . .
> I certainly/probably won't . . .
> I will/may/might be able to . . .
> I will/may/might have to . . .

1. If I spend it on a trip round the world
2. If I use it to start a business
3. If I share it with my family
4. If I invest it in government securities
5. If I spend it on private English lessons
6. If I stop work
7. If I buy a hotel
8. If I go on living exactly as before

5 Read the text, and choose conjunctions from the box to go in the gaps. (More than one answer may be possible.)

and	because	but	if	so	though	until	when

.....1..... I was a child I had violin lessons for six or seven years. Music gave me a lot of pleasure, and I sometimes used to dream of being a professional musician. But as time went on I realised that I would never reach that standard, mainly .....2..... I didn't have a good enough ear. .....3..... I gradually lost interest in the violin, and when I left school I stopped playing altogether. I may take up the violin again one of these days, ...4..... it will have to wait .....5..... I have time to practise properly.

Listening to music is a different matter. I go to concerts when I have time, and I often listen to music .....6..... I am working (.....7..... I sometimes find it hard to concentrate on music and work at the same time). My job involves quite a lot of driving, ...8..... I usually take a few cassettes with me to play in the car. My tastes are quite varied. I like a lot of classical music (particularly Bach, Handel, Beethoven and Stravinsky), ...9..... opera leaves me cold. I am very fond of modern jazz (especially Miles Davis), and I have a passion for British and American folk music. The one thing I really can't stand is pop music, especially .....10..... it's played loud.

6 Write about your own musical experience and tastes. Use words and expressions from Exercise 5.

"Wolfgang!"

7 Read this with a dictionary. Four sentences have been taken out and put at the end. Where should each one go?

One warm summer night in 1924, the cellist Beatrice Harrison went out to play her cello in the woods behind her cottage in Surrey, in the south of England.

After playing for some time in the moonlight, she paused. To her surprise, she heard a bird echoing her playing. (.....**1**.....) The sound was incredibly beautiful, and she knew that it could only be a nightingale.

(.....**2**.....) Beatrice Harrison could hardly believe what was happening: she was playing duets with a wild bird! It was an astonishing experience, and she wished that she could share her pleasure with other people.

At that time, broadcasting was just becoming popular, and many people in Europe had radios. Beatrice Harrison decided to try to persuade the BBC to set up their microphones in her garden.

(.....**3**.....) The BBC had never before tried an outside broadcast of this kind, and the distance between Beatrice Harrison's home and London made things more complicated. But the sound engineers made careful preparations, and one night in May 1924 everything was ready.

For a long time it seemed as if the nightingale was not going to come. (.....**4**.....) But suddenly, to everybody's relief, the wonderful liquid notes began to fill the night. The duet of the musician and the nightingale was heard in London, in Paris, even in Italy.

Several more broadcasts were made, and the following year HMV made a record of Beatrice and the Nightingale, which became one of the most successful records sold in the 1930s.

A. Beatrice Harrison played for nearly two hours with no reaction.
B. She started again, and the bird sang with her.
C. The next night, and nearly every night after that, the nightingale was there again.
D. With the technology of the time, this was no easy task.

Unit 9

B Audiences

1 Grammar revision: comparative and superlative adjectives. Copy and complete the table.

ADJECTIVE	COMPARATIVE	SUPERLATIVE	ADJECTIVE	COMPARATIVE	SUPERLATIVE
cold	colder	coldest	young	....	....
hot	hotter	hottest	happy	....	....
beautiful	more beautiful	most beautiful	easy	....	....
			late	....	....
long	....	....	nice	....	....
fast	....	....	intelligent	....	....
light	....	....	boring	....	....
big	....	....	good	....	....
sad	....	....	bad	....	....

2 Grammar revision: position of adverbs. Write sentences to say how much you like or dislike different kinds of music. Use the words and expressions in the box to help you. Examples:

I very much like jazz.
I particularly dislike Beethoven.

very much   particularly   especially
rather   quite

3 Grammar revision: position of adverbs. Add one of the expressions in the box to each sentence. Example:

My brother plays the trumpet brilliantly.

at the same time   brilliantly   perfectly
quickly   quite well   regularly   too slowly

1. My brother plays the trumpet.
2. I thought you sang that song.
3. It must be nice to play an instrument.
4. They played the last part.
5. I used to practise the violin when I was at school.
6. I don't understand how a pianist can think about both hands.
7. Try to sing that song backwards.

4 Do you know the English names of the musical notes? They are the letters of the alphabet A–G.

C   D   E   F   G   A   B

If you are interested in music, look up these words in your dictionary and learn them.

flat   sharp   major   minor   key   scale
tone   semitone   octave

5 Practise saying these words with the correct stress. Check the pronunciation and meaning in your dictionary.

symphony   instrument
trombone   violin   guitar
conductor   composer   concerto   sonata
clarinet

6 Read this with a dictionary.

Musical instruments 25,000 years old have been found in Hungary.

The longest musical instrument in the world is a Swiss alphorn which measures over 13 metres from end to end.

The biggest guitar in the world stands 2.6 metres tall and weighs 36 kilograms.

Some violins made by Antonio Stradivari (1644–1737) are worth over £1 million.

Wolfgang Amadeus Mozart wrote his last three symphonies in 42 days.

The American composer John Cage has written a piece of 'music' which consists of 4 minutes and 33 seconds of total silence.

The most frequently sung English song is *Happy Birthday to you.*

Between 1962 and 1978, Paul McCartney wrote 43 songs which sold a million or more records.

The famous British pianist Solomon gave his first public concert at the age of 8, playing the slow movement of the Tchaikowsky B♭ piano concerto. At the end of the performance he was given a tricycle, which he rode off the stage.

On his 100th birthday, the jazz musician Eubie Blake said, 'If I'd known I was gonna live this long I'd have taken better care of myself.'

THERE IS NO PRACTICE BOOK WORK FOR UNIT 10

Language

A Learning a language

1 Here is the beginning of a vocabulary network. Copy it, and put the words and expressions from the list in suitable places. Can you add some more?

adjectives   cloud   consonants   Greek   idea   intonation
Japanese   languages   prepositions   present perfect
run   simple past   stress   table   think

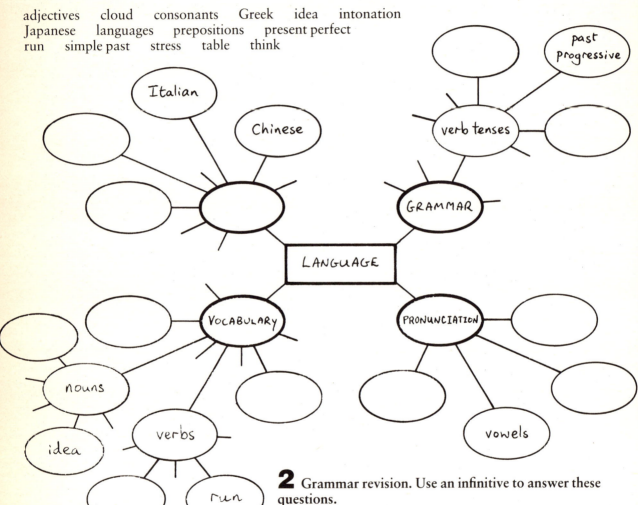

2 Grammar revision. Use an infinitive to answer these questions.

1. Why do tourists go to France?

   To see Paris.
   To visit Provence.

2. Why do tourists go to Italy/Spain/Greece/the USA/Egypt?
3. Why do people go to banks?
4. Why do people go to post offices?
5. Why do people go to airports?
6. Why do children go to school?
7. Why are you learning English?

3 Grammar revision. Can you copy and complete the lists of pronouns?

I	me	....	mine	....
you	....	his	....	
....	....	his	....	
....	....	its	-----	....
....	us		....	
....	....	yours	....	
....	....	....	themselves	

4 Grammar revision: irregular verbs. Write the infinitive, past and participle of each verb.

INFINITIVE	PAST	PARTICIPLE
buy	....	....
....	chose	....
....	....	drunk
fall	....	....
....	felt	....
....	....	forgotten
give	....	....
....	grew	....
....	....	heard
hide	....	....
....	hit	....
....	....	learnt
lend	....	....
....	let	....
lie	....	....
....	lost	....
....	....	meant
meet	....	....
....	paid	....
....	....	slept

5 This is the text of the talk from Exercises 5 and 6 of Student's Book Lesson 11A. Read it with a dictionary.

THE ORIGINS OF WRITING

Who invented writing?

The world's earliest writing system seems to have been used by the Sumerians, who lived in the Middle East, where Iraq is today. They had a kind of picture writing, with over 1,500 signs for different objects, numbers, and other ideas. The signs were written with a piece of wood on clay tablets, which were then baked to keep them hard and preserve the writing.

Where did the complicated Sumerian writing system come from? Did they invent it, or was it developed from an earlier, simpler writing system used by somebody else? Nobody knows the answer to this question, but archaeologists have not found an earlier writing system, although they have excavated thousands of sites in the Middle East.

The archaeologist Denise Schmandt-Besserat has an interesting theory. In an article in the journal *Scientific American*, she suggests that writing may have developed from the use of stones and other objects for accounting.

In many parts of the world, people use small objects – stones, pieces of wood, etc. – for keeping records and accounts. The Romans used stones, and their word for a small stone – calculus – has given us our word *calculate*. Small discs or balls are used in the Chinese abacus. And in Iraq, even today, shepherds use stones to keep count of their sheep.

Almost everywhere in the Middle East, archaeologists have found small objects made of clay. These objects are of several different shapes: for example, spheres, cones, discs, pyramids and cylinders. The earliest objects date from 10,500 years ago, at about the time when farming was beginning. It seems that the objects were tokens used for accounting. For instance, objects of a particular shape represented sheep. People used them to check the numbers and movements of their animals. If a lamb was born, another token was added; when an animal was killed, a token was taken away. When sheep were moved to another place, the tokens were put on a different shelf in the building where records were kept. Other objects represented other kinds of animals such as cattle or dogs, while still others stood for cloth, metals, oil and so on. Some represented numbers.

When the first cities grew up, these clay objects were used in a new way. If a farmer or cloth-maker sent animals or goods to the city, he sent with them a record to show what there was. For example, if he sent 48 sheep he would send along 48 of the tokens that represented sheep. So that nobody could steal any of the sheep, he put the 48 tokens in a hollow clay sphere, closed it up, put his personal seal – his signature – on the outside and baked it. The person who received his goods in the city would break open the sphere to check that everything was there.

Later, people had the idea of marking the outside of the clay sphere to show what tokens were inside, so that it was possible to check the goods even before breaking open the sphere. So on the outside of the sphere, they made pictures of the objects which were inside.

Later still, people realised that it was not necessary to go on using clay tokens – the pictures were just as good, and could be put on flat pieces of clay instead of spheres.

And as time went on, these pictures were used to write other kinds of messages besides business records, and more signs were invented. Writing had begun, and it soon spread all across Western Asia.

6 Look at Exercise 3 of Student's Book Lesson 11A. Choose one or more of the questions and write a few lines giving your opinion.

B Guess what the accents are

1 Word stress. Where do you think the main stress comes in each of the following words? Use a dictionary to check your answers.

vocabulary   pronunciation

language   expression   important
translation   consonant   intonation
conversation   ability   understand

Where does the main stress come in words that end in *-ation*?

2 Vocabulary revision. Can you match the countries and the languages? Can you add the names of any more countries with their languages?

Algeria   Australia   Austria   Brazil
Mexico   Norway   Pakistan
Uganda   Wales

Arabic   English   German
Norwegian   Portuguese   Spanish
Swahili   Urdu   Welsh

"I don't know anybody who says 'It is I'."

3 Spelling. Some of these words have one or more letters missing. What are they, and where do they go?

fortunatly	making	interview
fortunately	peple	Mediteranean
	bargin	responsbility
organisation	suceful	disapear
(correct)	pronunciation	memry

4 Can you match the British words and their American equivalents? Do you know any other words which are different in British and American English?

GB
angry   autumn   engine   film   first floor
flat   ground floor   handbag   holiday
ill   lift   mad   maths   motorway
pavement   petrol   post   purse
reverse-charge call   road surface   shop
sweets   tap   taxi   toilet   trousers

US
apartment   cab   candy   coin purse
collect call   crazy   elevator   fall   faucet
first floor   freeway   gas   mad   mail
math   motor   movie   pants   pavement
purse   restroom   second floor   sick
sidewalk   store   vacation

5 Can you add five words to each of these groups? Do you know what the different kinds of words are called? The names are in the box.

1. sit, get, write, belong, . . .
2. hotel, film, idea, cow, . . .
3. green, heavy, wrong, late, . . .
4. on, by, with, . . .
5. fast, easily, now, there, . . .
6. although, after, when, . . .

| adjective   adverb   conjunction   noun |
| preposition   verb |

6 Write a few paragraphs about your experience of learning English (and other languages, if you have learnt any others). Use words and expressions from Unit 11 of the Student's Book.

54

7 Read one or both of these texts.

GERMAN-FRENCH-JAPANESE NIGHT SONG
There is a famous poem by the German writer Goethe, entitled *Nachtgedicht* ('Night Poem'). Roughly translated into English, it goes:

Above all the mountain peaks
Is peace.
In all the treetops
You can hear
Hardly a breath of wind.
The small birds are silent in the forest.
Just wait, and soon
You too will be at peace.

In 1902 a Japanese translation of Goethe's poem was published. Nine years later a French writer translated this into his own language, believing it to be an original Japanese poem. And finally, a German editor translated the French version back into German and published it in a magazine under the title *Japanisches Nachtlied* ('Japanese Night Song'). It now went roughly as follows:

There is silence in the jade pavilion.
Crows fly noiselessly
to snow-covered cherry trees in the moonlight.
I sit
and weep.

THANK YOU VERY MATCH

Dear sir,

Im writing this letter in a no god english, i cant this no perfect. I must say you very, very thank you very match for the sleeping in your Rooms. We was in the Aoust with Mihail in St Germain and have Visit Paris by Day and Night. Its was very nice and we have saved us Monay for this reason. Your ought to coming Germany, my house is open for you.

(Letter from a German to an Englishman who had lent him a flat in Paris)

"Phrase-book!"

Unit 12

News

A The voice of democracy

1 Look at the examples and then choose the correct tenses in the other sentences.

1. 'Look! (*I found*/*I've found*) a ten-pound note!' 'It's probably mine. Where (*did you find*/*have you found*) it?'
2. 'Alice (*bought*/*has bought*) a new car.' 'Really? Where (*did she get*/*has she got*) the money?'
3. 'I'm sorry. I (*broke*/*'ve broken*) a cup.' 'How (*did you manage*/*have you managed*) to do that?'
4. My father (*just had*/*has just had*) a car accident, but he (*wasn't*/*hasn't been*) badly hurt.
5. News (*just came in*/*has just come in*) of an earthquake in Southern Mangrovia. According to first reports, the quake (*struck*/*has struck*) just after midnight last night.
6. 'Mummy! Look what (*I did*/*I've done*)!' 'Oh, my God! What (*did you do*/*have you done*) that for?'
7. 'Did you know Henry (*went*/*has gone*) to California?' 'Oh, yes? He (*probably wanted*/*has probably wanted*) to get away from Bill for a bit.'
8. ('*What happened*/'*What's happened*) here?' 'It looks as if he (*came*/*has come*) round the corner too fast.'
9. 'You know those young trees we (*planted*/*have planted*)? They (*all died*/*have all died*).' 'You probably (*didn't water*/*haven't watered*) them enough.'

2 Which tense would you probably use with these time expressions – simple past or present perfect? Examples:

yesterday: simple past – *I saw Gill yesterday.*
all this year: present perfect – *She's been ill all this year.*

last week	once upon a time
ten years ago	for the last few weeks
since Tuesday	after we got married
all my life	since we got married
when I first met you	during my childhood
the day before yesterday	up to now

3 Think of explanations for these situations. Use the present perfect progressive. Examples:

SITUATION	EXPLANATION
She's all wet.	*She's been swimming.*
Her feet hurt.	*She's been dancing.*

Her shoes are dirty.
She's got paint on her hands.
She's got flour on her hands.
She's got oil on her hands.
She's got toothpaste on her chin.
She's sweating.
She's tired.
Her cheeks are wet.
She's lost her voice.
She's just going to the post office.

4 How long is it since you've done these things? Use the structure *I haven't . . . since/for . . .* Examples:

eaten an ice cream – *I haven't eaten an ice cream for weeks.*
been shopping – *I haven't been shopping since yesterday.*

travelled by train	fallen in love
read a novel	been ill
been to the cinema	been in hospital
played football	done an examination
stayed up all night	spoken to a policeman

5 Contrastive stress. Which of the words in italics has the strongest stress? Can you say the sentences?

1. 'It's ten past two.' 'Your watch is wrong. It's *ten past three.*'
2. I said I wanted a *glass of milk*, not a glass of water.
3. She asked for hot milk, but the waiter brought her *cold milk*.
4. 'Who's the girl in red?' 'You mean the one in the red skirt or the one in the *red sweater*?'
5. Some people think that *brown sugar* is better for you than white.
6. 'When are we seeing Peter – is it Thursday?' 'No, Tuesday – we're seeing *Jim and Elsa on Thursday*.'
7. 'Shall we look at the plans before dinner?' 'I'd prefer *after dinner*, if you don't mind.'

"I've been replaced by a doormat."

6 Read the following letter and then do Exercise 7.

---

18 Marble Lane
Penygroes
Gwynedd
North Wales
LL6 7AQ

14 July 1985

Dear Bernard,

Thanks for your letter. It was good to hear from you and get all your news.

We've just started work on the new building. It will take approximately six months to get it finished, if all goes well. It's an exciting project, and we're all very pleased that we got the contract.

I've found a nice place to live - just outside the village, on the edge of a small lake. It's an old house, but it's in very good condition, and extremely comfortable. There's plenty of spare room, so why don't you and Janice come up one weekend?

The only problem here is the weather. According to the locals, this is the wettest summer in living memory, and I can quite believe it. It's rained every day since I got here, and it shows no sign of stopping.

Still, in spite of the weather I'm enjoying myself. The people here are very friendly, and I've been elected to the darts team in the local pub. Apparently they've lost their last sixteen matches, and they're hoping that a bit of outside talent may improve their record.

I'll try to get down to London sometime in the next couple of months, but I don't think I'll have time for a bit. I'm going to have to spend at least three weeks here getting the work and the house organised before I can get away.

No more news for the moment. Write soon and let me know what's going on back in the big city.

Love to Janice,

Yours,

---

7 Write a letter giving some news about yourself to a friend or relation. Use the following 'skeleton' as a basis. You can change the order of words, and make any other changes you need to, but you must use plenty of the words and expressions in the skeleton, and some other words and expressions from Exercise 6.

ADDRESS
DATE

Dear . . . ,

Thanks . . .
I've just started . . .
It will take approximately . . . to . . .

I've found . . .
Why don't you . . . ?

The only problem . . .
According to . . .
I can quite believe it.

In spite of . . .
It's/I've . . . every day since . . .

I'll try . . .
but I don't think . . .
I'm going to have to . . .

No more news for the moment.
Write soon and . . .

Love/Yours,

B The Swiss have voted

1 Vocabulary. Put in words from the box.

available	average	demonstration
details	efficient	figures	inflation
opposition	policies	prompt	reported
violence

1. According to government ....,
   unemployment is down by 13%, and
   .... has fallen to 3%.
2. The .... weekly wage has gone up by 80%
   since 1980.
3. The government say that this is due to their
   economic ....
4. Mr Gresk, leader of the Trade Union
   Confederation, has criticised Fantasian
   management for not being .... enough.
5. There was a large .... against educational
   reforms yesterday. It was mainly peaceful, but
   there were a few outbreaks of .... at the
   end, following speeches by .... leaders.
   However, ... action by police stopped the
   fighting and restored order. Several people are
   .... to have been hurt, but no further
   .... are .... for the moment.

2 Vocabulary revision. Can you match the words and the pictures?

catch   climb   dance   drop   fall   hit   jump   kick   lift   pull   push   roll   run
slip   swing   throw   trip   turn   walk

3 Pronounce these expressions. Be careful to join the end of the first word to the beginning of the next without a pause.

without talking   book cover   stand back
could drive   red telephone first post
stop playing   sit down   next Tuesday
card table

4 Join the beginnings and ends together to make sensible sentences.

BEGINNINGS	ENDS
Although I loved her,	I took an aspirin.
When it started raining,	you won't arrive before dark.
Unless you start now,	I switched on the radio.
After I'd finished the housework,	I decided not to see her again.
Before you start your new job,	I went to the pub.
Until you've seen it yourself,	write and tell me how you are.
Because I had a headache,	you ought to have a holiday.
As soon as I got up,	you won't believe how big it is.
If you have time,	I closed the windows.

5 Write one or more items for an imaginary radio or TV news programme. Include some of the words and expressions in the box.

according to	at least	approximately	available	average	bright	cloudy
collision	demonstration	details	due to	efficient	figures	inflation
in spite of	investigate	neutral	opposition	policy	pop star	prompt
report	smash	suspect	violence	vote	wreckage	

6 Read some or all of these news items with a dictionary. (This is the text of the broadcast in Exercise 2 of Student's Book Lesson 12B.)

The Swiss have voted overwhelmingly today to retain their neutrality by rejecting government proposals to join the United Nations. The government and most of the major parties wanted Switzerland to become the 160th member of the UN, but more than 75% of voters preferred to keep their country in isolation, maintaining the neutrality internationally acknowledged since 1815.

Four black people have been shot and killed by police in South Africa. Beatrice Hollier sends this report.
    'The daily police unrest report shows three black miners shot and killed by police in a mining district near Johannesburg. Another seven miners were injured. And in Soweto, outside Johannesburg, police shot and killed a man they said was part of a crowd burning houses. In Cape Town and Port Elizabeth, thousands are gathering for the funerals of alleged nationalist guerrillas killed in a police shoot-out recently. Beatrice Hollier, IRN, Johannesburg.'

Raiders have smashed their way into the Wiltshire home of pop star Peter Sarstedt, and got away with ten thousand pounds' worth of antiques, musical equipment and paintings. Sarstedt, best known for his song 'Where did you go to, my lovely?' is now returning to help his family clear up the mess left by the raiders at his home near Devizes. His wife Joanna says he's had to halt work on an album and a film.

Police in Swindon are investigating a case of suspected arson following a fire in Brew Street last night. Damage estimated at £500 was caused when flames swept through a garage at number 44. And damage in the region of £500 was caused last night in Marlowe Avenue in Swindon, when a dustbin was hurled through the front window of Scratchley's newsagents. Police were called to the scene just after one o'clock.

Two men have been killed and six people hurt in a collision in North London between a police car and a minicar. Three of the injured are police officers. They were on an emergency call driving through Maida Vale when the mini crossed the path of their vehicle. All six of those hurt have been taken to St Mary's Hospital in Paddington in West London.

Two Britons are tunnelling into the wreckage of a collapsed hotel in Singapore to rescue a woman and her son. The rescuers are crawling through gaps in the concrete rubble of the hotel's basement car park. They are being helped by an Irishman and four Singapore workers with high-pressure concrete-cutting water jets. The Britons are Michael Prendergast from Newcastle on Tyne and Brian Power from Lancashire. They both work on Singapore's new underground railway project. Seven bodies have so far been pulled from the wreckage of the New World Hotel. A British passport has been found in the rubble.

And the weather forecast for the west now. Becoming brighter after a cloudy start to the day, a little drizzle in places. This afternoon, sunshine in most parts, but still cloudy on high ground. Top temperatures round about twelve Celsius, that's a warm 54 Fahrenheit, the wind southerly and light to moderate. Tonight's overcast again, fog in places, rain and drizzle likely:

7 Try the crossword.

[crossword grid]

ACROSS

1. No further details are .... for the moment.
6. From Egypt.
8. From a lower place to a higher place.
9. Like a mouse, but bigger.
11. You put it in an ashtray.
12. Halfway from your feet to your hips.
13. Road in a town.
15. Please give your name, address, ... and occupation.
16. She was .... tired that she couldn't even stand up.
17. 'Could you do me a favour?' '............ depends.'
19. The opposite of *come*.
20. Prices are going up fast because we have a high rate of ....

DOWN

1. He's 20, you're 23 and I'm 32. Our .... age is 25.
2. I don't want .... to eat, thanks.
3. I'm going to write a .... to my MP about the government's immigration policies.
4. Bedclothes.
5. Political group which is not in power.
7. Do you cook by .... or electricity?
10. Not there.
14. The part of a plant that grows downwards.
15. I usually go running .... lunchtime.
17. I'll ring you again .... a few days.
18. Let me know .... I can give you any help.
19. Prices usually seem to .... up faster than earnings.

(*Solution on page 137.*)

"*The practice of astrology took a major step toward achieving credibility today when, as predicted, everyone born under the sign of Scorpio was run over by an egg lorry.*"

Fears

A The Lonely One

1 Put a word from the box into each blank. You may have to change verb tenses or make plurals; some words may be used more than once.

around	dangerous	drugstore	lean	lonely	maybe	promise	purse	single
strange	stranger	terrify	waste					

I had a really ....1.... experience the other night. It was about 10.30, ...2.... 11 o'clock; I had a headache, and there were no aspirins in the house, so I decided to walk down to Abel's, the all-night ....3.... on Montrose Boulevard. My brother says I shouldn't walk by myself after dark, that it's ....4...., but I'm careful and don't take any unnecessary chances. I keep my money in a pocket, not in a ....5....; I carry my keys in such a way as to be able to hurt somebody with them if necessary; I walk briskly and confidently. Anyway, Abel's is only ....6.... the corner from my apartment. I refuse to let myself be ....7.... into staying inside the house after dark just because I'm a ....8.... woman.

Well, anyway, when I walked out of the apartment building I noticed a ....9.... ....10.... against a parked car about thirty feet down the street, in the opposite direction from where I was going – kind of odd, but I didn't ....11.... any time worrying about it. I went to the ....12.... and got the aspirins, and spent a little time talking to Juanita behind the counter. She gets pretty ....13.... here so far from her family; and working the night shift doesn't help, as far as meeting people socially goes.

After I made Juanita ....14.... to come by for lunch whenever she felt like it, I headed for home and a good book. Little did I suspect that I wasn't going to get much reading done that night.

As I turned to go up the steps to my apartment house, I noticed something moving on the ground where the ....15.... had been standing before. I carefully went a little closer, and realised that it was the ....16.... – minus quite a bit of blood. I tore his shirt for bandages to stop the worst of the bleeding, ran home to call an ambulance and the police, and then came back outside to keep him company. He said something about Milton or Melton, and something else that I didn't understand, again and again until the ambulance came.

2 Grammar revision. Put one of the prepositions from the box ...into... each blank.

around	down	into	off	onto	out of	over	through	towards	up

1. Drive .... Cirencester, but turn off before you get there: watch for the sign that says 'Upton' and 'The Lamberts', to the left.
2. Let's just climb .... the wall – otherwise we'll have to walk miles.
3. I'm always a bit afraid of falling .... these stairs – they're really not very safe.
4. You can see .... the hedge now, but in the summer it makes a solid green wall.
5. Everyone else in the compartment got .... the train at Dundee, so I was alone for the last part of the journey.
6. We carried our cameras and binoculars all the way .... the mountain, and then it was so misty we couldn't see a thing.
7. You remember I was telling you about my old school friend Chris last week? Well, I saw him walk .... one of the buildings across the street from my office today! He noticed me at the same time and crossed the street to say hello.
8. It will be easier to sweep and mop in here if we put the chairs .... the tables first.
9. I didn't know which door she would be coming out of, so I walked .... the building several times.

3 Grammar revision. *-ing* form, infinitive with *to*, or infinitive without *to*? Put each verb into the correct form.

1. .... in a room where I can't see the exit makes me a bit uncomfortable. (*be*)
2. I don't want .... so frightened, but I can't help it. (*be*)
3. My doctor told me .... about something else while the plane was taking off, but it didn't do much good. (*think*)
4. I can't drive through a tunnel without .... about what would happen if the roof fell in. (*worry*)
5. For all my brothers, ... through the long tunnel under the ship channel was always something .... (*drive, look forward to*)
6. When I saw the snake, I just couldn't .... (*move*)
7. I used to be terrified of .... in front of a lot of people. (*speak*)
8. I had to ask my wife .... the spider out of the bath. (*get*)
9. I'm a bit better if I've got something .... my mind. (*occupy*)
10. I always ask people .... me stand near the door in a lift. (*let*)
11. It may .... it easier if you try to imagine what the other person feels like. (*make*)
12. My fears are a bit easier to deal with now that I have someone .... about them. (*talk to*)

4 Where are the stresses? Copy the text and underline the stressed syllables. In some cases more than one stress pattern is possible.

The first time it ever happened to me was in Borneo, when I was diving off a reef for shells. I was working up there for an oil company for six weeks once, and I used to dive off a reef from a shallow boat. And once I went so far from the boat – I was enjoying myself so much I wasn't looking where I was going, and I suddenly looked down. The reef that I'd been diving on just dropped away completely, and I couldn't see the bottom, and I panicked.

LOST PROPERTY

"Yes, as a matter of fact we have."

5 Read these with a dictionary.

Men fear death as children fear to go in the dark; and as that natural fear in children is increased with tales, so is the other.

(Francis Bacon)

The only thing we have to fear is fear itself.

(Franklin D. Roosevelt)

In the future days, which we seek to make secure, we look forward to a world founded upon four essential human freedoms.

The first is freedom of speech and expression – everywhere in the world.

The second is freedom of every person to worship God in his own way – everywhere in the world.

The third is freedom from want . . .

And the fourth is freedom from fear.

(Franklin D. Roosevelt)

Cowards die many times before their deaths;
The valiant never taste of death but once.
Of all the wonders that I yet have heard
It seems to me most strange that men should fear;
Seeing that death, a necessary end,
Will come when it will come.

(Shakespeare: *Julius Caesar*)

Let us begin anew – remembering on both sides that civility is not a sign of weakness, and sincerity is always subject to proof. Let us never negotiate out of fear. But let us never fear to negotiate.

(John F. Kennedy)

Through the Jungle very softly flits a shadow and a sigh –
He is Fear, O Little Hunter, he is Fear!

(Rudyard Kipling)

It is a miserable state of mind to have few things to desire and many things to fear.

(Francis Bacon)

Alas! the love of women! it is known
To be a lovely and a fearful thing!

(Lord Byron)

You may take the most gallant sailor, the most intrepid airman, or the most audacious soldier, put them at a table together – what do you get? The sum of their fears.

(Winston Churchill)

As for me, I see no such great cause why I should either be fond to live or fear to die. I have had good experience of this world, and I know what it is to be a subject and what to be a sovereign. Good neighbours I have had, and I have met with bad: and in trust I have found treason.

(Queen Elizabeth I)

6 Write about one of the following subjects. Use some words and expressions from Student's Book Lesson 13A.

1. Write about a time in your life when you were very frightened – either as a child or as an adult.
2. Do you know anyone who is very afraid of something, like spiders or heights? Describe the fear, how it makes the person feel and act, and what he or she has tried to do about it.

3. Write some advice for a person who is afraid of small closed spaces, or speaking in public, or aeroplanes.

"A word of advice, Arthur: no one ever solved his problems by running away."

B I was terrified

1 Vocabulary exploration. Divide the words in the box into four lists, using the titles below.

Phobias
Causes of phobias
Emotional states
Physical symptoms

agoraphobia   bothered   busy shops
can't breathe properly   claustrophobia
damp hands   fear of heights   frightened
ladders   lifts   mice   mountains   panic
restaurants   scared   shaking   shivering
spiders   terrified   tunnels

2 Grammar revision. Put in the right word.

1. I'm not very .... in poetry.
   (*interested / interesting*)
2. There's a really .... film on TV tonight.
   (*interested / interesting*)
3. Do you find bullfighting ....?
   (*excited / exciting*)
4. I went to a bullfight once, and I was ....
   (*disgusted / disgusting*)
5. Penny and I went to the opera last night. I'm afraid I was very .... (*bored / boring*)
6. Psychology is a .... subject.
   (*fascinated / fascinating*)
7. I'm .... to see you again.
   (*delighted / delighting*)

"*Not to worry, sir, most people get a little nervous the first time they crash.*"

3 Vocabulary revision. Label as many of these objects as you can.

4 Look quickly at these texts and choose one to read with a dictionary. Try not to look up words whose meanings you can guess.

The mystery phobia

Jane Bruff was a 37-year-old married English woman who kept a fruit shop. Quite out of the blue she began to suffer 'attacks' of very rapid heartbeat which made her feel alarmed and panicky. She was able to put up with these funny turns at home, but when she began to get them in the street, she really began to worry. Eventually the fear of having an attack in public forced her to take a taxi even for the two-hundred-yard trip down the street to her fruit shop. If possible she preferred to stay indoors, and she became very anxious at the thought of having to step too far outside the familiar safety of her home.

Jane had not kept her suffering to herself; she had consulted her GP and a heart specialist. She was pre-scribed Sotalol, a drug used to correct abnormalities of the heart, but it did her no good.

Her persistent distress, combined with the fact that she showed no sign of having an identifiable organic problem, only succeeded in getting her labelled as a 'problem patient'. Her specialist eventually told her there was nothing wrong with her heart and took her off the Sotalol.

Fortunately for Jane, a hospital consultant in her area had recently taken an interest in food allergy and had decided to test whether or not it was a genuine disease. He had talked about it to his colleagues, and Jane was referred to his clinic. He found out that Jane was a 'tea fiend', drinking a dozen or more cups of tea a day. He tested her on several different occasions by putting a plastic tube down her throat (so she could not taste what was going into her stomach), and poured either coffee, tea, or water down it from an opaque syringe (so Jane could not see what was going into the tube). Every time tea or coffee was tested, after two and a half hours, Jane's heartbeat suddenly shot up from the regular normal 70 beats a minute to 250 beats, an alarming rate, which brought back her old feeling of panic.

Jane was asked to give up coffee and tea. It worked; within a very short time she had lost all her symptoms, was happy to walk down the street, and had returned to her job and a normal social life.

(from *Eating and Allergy* by Robert Eagle – adapted)

Fear is necessary

Not only is fear a very normal emotion, but it is also an essential emotion. To be totally without fear is to be in serious danger. Fear is an essential defence mechanism.

Fear is made up of an emotional feeling and a number of bodily changes. If we come face to face with a man wildly waving a hatchet we are likely to experience the emotion we describe as fear, and at the same time our hearts will start to race, our breathing will accelerate, and we may turn pale and sweat. We may experience an unpleasant sinking sensation in the stomach, weakness of the muscles, and trembling of the limbs. We may have a desire to micturate, defecate, or vomit, and may in fact carry out some of these functions. These physical changes have been described as the 'fight or flight phenomenon', and they are the body's preparation for either of these actions. An increased heart rate pumps more blood to the muscles, so they are ready for action. An increase in breathing ensures that more oxygen is available for the same use. Sweating makes it more difficult for us to be grabbed, while making our hair stand up would be protective if we were still well covered with hair. For human beings getting our hair erect is rather a waste of time, as unfortunately are other body changes that have been described. Weakness of the muscles and shaking is not much use for either fight or flight and neither are vomiting, defecating, or micturating. It appears that for one reason or another the body's mechanism to deal with emergencies sometimes goes wrong; and this is not confined to human beings. Other animals also become paralysed with fear and actually die from it.

(from *Fears and Phobias* by Dr Tony Whitehead – adapted)

FIRST DAY AT SCHOOL

A millionbillionwillion miles from home
Waiting for the bell to go. (To go where?)
Why are they all so big, other children?
So noisy? So much at home they
must have been born in uniform
Lived all their lives in playgrounds
Spent the years inventing games
that don't let me in. Games
that are rough, that swallow you up.

And the railings.
All around, the railings.
Are they to keep out wolves and monsters?
Things that carry off and eat children?
Things you don't take sweets from?
Perhaps they're to stop us getting out
Running away from the lessins. Lessin.
What does a lessin look like?
Sounds small and slimy.
They keep them in glassrooms.
Whole rooms made out of glass. Imagine.

I wish I could remember my name
Mummy said it would come in useful.
Like wellies. When there's puddles.
Yellowwellies. I wish she was here.
I think my name is sewn on somewhere
Perhaps the teacher will read it for me.
Tea-cher. The one who makes the tea.

(Roger McGough)

lessin: lesson
glassroom: classroom
wellies: boots made of rubber

5 Read this letter to an 'agony aunt' – a person who has a page in a magazine for answering letters from people who have problems. Then write a letter to an agony aunt about your own real or imaginary fear or phobia.

Dear Marion,

I have a horrible problem, and I hope you can help me with it. I have been going out with a wonderful woman for a year now. We get on very well in all sorts of ways, and I am very much in love with her. I am sure I want to marry her. But I can't bring myself to pop the question. I have made up my mind to ask her several times, but I always get scared at the last minute. I have spent hours making up romantic speeches, and then when the time comes I can't get anything out. I go red, I begin to sweat, my mouth goes dry, and I just can't speak. I am just so afraid she will say no. What can I do? Please help me.

C.G., Hemel Hempstead

"No, thank you. Last time I went over the top I nearly got killed."

Politics

A Labour and Conservative

1 Put one of these into each blank: *because, because of, although, in spite of.* Sometimes more than one answer can be correct.

1. .... we are sure our party will lose the local election, we think it is important to have a candidate.
2. Celia is a superb chairperson, ... she is very good at sharing responsibility.
3. .... very bad weather conditions, over 85 per cent of the registered voters actually voted.
4. The newspapers seem to think that Labour won .... their defence policy.
5. Some politicians seem to succeed not .... they are effective politicians, but .... the relationships they build with important people in the party.
6. Lawson has made a very good county councillor, ... he was not at all involved in politics until he was in his forties.
7. The Conservatives managed to keep the majority on the council .... predictions that they would lose it.

2 Pronunciation. Copy the words and underline the stressed syllables. Check with your dictionary to make sure you are right, and pronounce the words.

candidate   civil service   civil servant   represent   Conservative   physical   politician
intelligence   relationship   organisation   successful   economics   political   responsible

3 Read the article; as you read, write your answers to the questions. Only use a dictionary if you are really stuck.

DEFENCE AND POVERTY
On present trends Britain will, just after the turn of the century, be the poorest nation in the whole of Europe apart from Albania. But at least, on present policy, it will have Trident to defend its increasingly rundown and divided society.

This is the result of British policy making since 1945, with its emphasis on the symbols of great power and status. The demands of the defence community have continually been put before the needs of the rest of society.

1. Do you think the author of this article is in favour of spending large sums of money on defence?
2. Why do you think the author speaks of a 'divided' society?

On the latest figures Britain spends 5½ per cent of its national wealth on defence compared with 4 per cent in France, just over 3 per cent in Germany and just under 3 per cent in Italy. The pattern has been the same for the last 30 years, as Britain has tied up more of its resources unproductively in the defence field than any of our competitors.

But what would happen if Britain were to reduce its defence expenditure to the level of say Germany and Italy? This would involve fundamental changes in policy, such as ending any pretence at having a world-wide Navy, together with huge cuts in the equipment programme and buying more equipment from abroad.

3. Who are some of Britain's competitors? What do you think they are competing for?
4. Why do you think Britain maintains a world-wide Navy?

The extra government spending that would be possible on schools, hospitals and schemes to reduce unemployment would be massive; but so would the major dislocation in huge areas of British industry. Unfortunately for those who want to change defence policy towards a more realistic structure and at the same time to improve British economic performance, the military-industrial complex is extremely powerful and includes not just military planners and industrial bosses but also trade unions and a huge number of jobs, probably as many as 800,000.

5. Why are some trade union leaders against spending less on defence?

Is there no way out of this dilemma? Some have suggested that it should be possible to wind down the defence industries and redeploy the effort to civil work just as was done after 1945. The problem is that then it was easy to demobilise the forces and rebuild civilian industry because there was a vast demand for its products after wartime shortages, and massive new programmes in areas like housing to employ ex-servicemen. And the government had enough power over the economy to control the rate of transition.

6. Was there big growth in civilian industry in your country after the Second World War?

To undertake a similar programme now, when there are nearly 4 million unemployed, in the hope that somehow new demand for British products will emerge, would be economic and political suicide. But what about starting with the industrial base – the research and development (R and D) effort? Britain puts more of its R and D money into the defence field than any other country, including the US. The latest figures show that almost 30 per cent of British R and D spending is on defence compared with 23 per cent in the US.

In Germany it is about 6 per cent and in Japan about ½ per cent. In Britain far too much of our best scientific effort is going into new military equipment and not enough into developing new products that might help revitalise the economy.

7. If you were Prime Minister of Britain, would you try and reduce the amount of money Britain spends on military research and development?
8. Why do you think Germany and Japan spend so little on military R and D?

Past experience suggests that just gradually cutting back on military spending will get nowhere. A major re-organisation of parts of the economy would be involved, and today's British industry could not carry out this reorganisation without government intervention. This sort of programme in today's circumstances can only be achieved by much greater state control of the whole process.

But is there any sign that a Labour government is prepared to face all the problems that such a policy involves?

9. Do you think government should have a lot of control over private industry?

(abridged from an article by Clive Ponting)

Trident: a type of nuclear missile

4 Copy the four lists, and find some more words to add to each of them. Look back at Lesson 14A in the Student's Book if necessary.

POLITICAL INSTITUTIONS
Parliament
House of Representatives (USA)
party
county council
....
....

POLITICAL PARTIES
Conservative
....
....

PEOPLE IN POLITICS
MP
candidate
....
....

OTHER POLITICAL CONCEPTS
represent
democracy
....
....

"Look, dear . . . it's the smaller tax bill the mayor promised us."

"Actually, it surprises me that a man like you doesn't hold political office."

Unit 14

B Neither left nor right

1 Grammar revision. Put in *be going to* or *will/'ll*.

1. Look out – we .... crash!
2. 'There's the doorbell.' 'I .... go.'
3. We promise that if you vote for us we .... double your income in twelve months.
4. Would you excuse me? I .... have a bath.
5. If you say that again I .... hit you.
6. The next train to arrive at platform six .... be the delayed seven thirty-two service for Bristol.
7. I wonder what she .... do with that hammer.
8. 'Can somebody answer the phone?' 'I ....'

2 Grammar revision. Write the contracted forms. Examples:

he is   *he's*

has not   *hasn't*

cannot   will not   she will   we have
they would   I had   does not   it will
I am   they are   might not   they will

3 Vocabulary revision. Match the adjectives and the nouns. (Some adjectives can go with more than one noun.) Can you add some more words and expressions to do with the weather?

heavy	sunshine
thick	temperatures
deep	wind
loud	hailstones
brilliant	snow
enormous	rain
strong	fog
bright	lightning
high	thunder

4 Imagine that you are the leader of a new political party. Write a few sentences about your party's policies.

5 Read the quotations with a dictionary.

'The Conservative Party must not be afraid of new or even of old ideas.'

(*The Times*)

'Lord Trenchard . . . has made his first speech in the House of Lords after 21 years' membership. His theme was Industrial Democracy. He didn't much care for the idea.'

(*Police Magazine*)

'Jill says she doesn't believe in all that Women's Lib stuff. "I want a man to look after me, to make a fuss of me," she says. "I don't have any political views either. I always vote Conservative."'

(*The Daily Mirror*)

'Sir Keith Joseph . . . last night spelled out the kind of Tory party he wanted to see: "We need more inequality in order to eliminate poverty."'

(*The Guardian*)

'The automatic flushing system of a gents' toilet in Totnes will be stopped when the Queen visits the town on 27 July – so that the noise does not disturb the Royal party. It has also been suggested that guests should stand in a semi-circle – to hide the entrance.'

(*The Sunday Pictorial*)

If I had a vote, I'd vote for the christmas Party

Politicians are people who tell other people to go to war

My auntie took me to the Joo and we saw too politishuns.

Why cant you vote for Love?

Two Politicians loving each other.

(from *Vote for Love*, compiled by Nanette Newman)

69

Schooldays

A I don't like playtime . . .

1 Vocabulary revision. Find words from the two lists that belong together. Example:

singing songs

asking   doing   drawing   listening to   making
playing   reading   singing   solving   telling
watching   working   writing

books   games   hard   letters   maths   pictures
plans   problems   questions   songs   stories
the radio   TV

2 Grammar revision. Put in *each*, *all*, *some*, *any*, *no* or *none*.

1. The teacher is careful to give .... time to ....
   child during the day.
2. .... children are a bit noisy, but most of them
   behave quite well, and there are .... serious
   discipline problems.
3. .... of the children can read and do simple maths,
   but .... of them still find it difficult to write.
4. The teacher would like to use microcomputers for
   maths, but there aren't .... in her classroom – in
   fact, there are .... in the school.
5. .... child has his or her own likes and dislikes.
6. Peggy likes .... the things they do at school.
7. Ben doesn't like .... of the school activities at all.

3 Grammar revision. Put in *there is, there was, there has been, there will be* etc.

1. Do you think .... a teachers' strike next week?
2. Why .... a dustbin in the living room?
3. .... two policemen at the back door. They say they
   want to see you.
4. When I got home, ... a letter from Charlie on the
   doormat.
5. Quick! Phone for an ambulance! .... an accident!
6. How many general elections .... since the war?
7. I used to enjoy cycling when I was younger, but
   ....n't so many cars then.
8. If food was properly distributed .... enough for
   everybody.

4 Spelling. Make adverbs. Examples:

quick *quickly*

nice *nicely*

easy *easily*

final *finally*

possible *possibly*

complete   definite   extreme   happy
heavy   hopeful   idle   kind   light
probable   real   slow   total

5 How do you feel about the subjects in the box? Use one of these expressions in each answer (but write more if you want to).

I really enjoy . . .
I'm extremely interested in . . .
I'm fascinated by . . .
I'm quite interested in . . .
I'd like to know more about . . .
I don't know anything about . . .
I've always wanted to learn something
   about . . .
I'm not very interested in . . .
I'm not in the least interested in . . .
I don't much like . . .
I don't like . . . at all.
I'm bored by . . .
I hate . . .
I think . . . is a complete waste of time.
I used to like . . . , but I've lost interest in it.
I used to think . . . was boring, but now I'm
   getting interested in it.

archaeology   art   biology
classical music   computing
cooking   economics   folk dancing
history   maths   philosophy
poetry   pop music   psychology
religion   wild life

6 Read this with a dictionary. (It is the transcript of the interview from Exercise 6 of Student's Book Lesson 15A.)

'OK, Louise. How about you? How do you feel about school?'

''S all right, erm, I like some bits of it, and I don't like other bits.'

'Which bits do you like, and which bits don't you like?'

'Er, you know, you like having your friends, and some of the teachers are all right – some of them – but, erm, I like some lessons, but some are really boring, and they don't do anything you like. And if you don't understand it then some teachers don't explain anything. 'S really boring.'

'Which lessons do you like?'

'English, and drama.'

'And which ones don't you like?'

'Physics. Maths.'

'OK.'

'And do you like school?'

'No.'

'Good. Why not?'

'It's boring . . . The teachers are all right, some of them, but the lessons, they just yabber on all the time, and nobody ever listens to them. So, they think that they're teaching, you know, but they ain't.'

'How – how would you – how would you change it if you – if you had the power to change something, how would you change it?'

'Blow it up.'

(Laughter)

'OK – are – are you s – do you think that kids your age shouldn't have to go to school, is that what you're saying?'

'Yeah, but the school that we go to, it ain't worth going to. It's – a dump. It's – the teachers – some of the teachers that are there are all right, they talk to you like you're normal, but some of the teachers there still treat you like a little kid – think that you should sit down and just be quiet while listening to them. But you don't, 'cause they're boring. 'Cause they are.'

'OK.'

'How about you, Liz?'

'Erm, school's OK, sometimes, and sometimes it isn't. I don't like it when they yabber on about exams, and they keep on at you for not doing your homework. Erm, I don't like some teachers, and I like some teachers – I like my English teacher, she's nice. But I hate my maths teacher and my physics teacher.'

'Why?'

'Well, they, they don't like me.'

'Kevin. And do you like school?'

'No.'

'Tell me about it.'

'Boring. As he – as Michael said. Erm, I mean, most of the time the teachers are on strike anyway. So, ha. There's no point in going to school.'

'Erm – is there anything about school you like?'

'Er – no.'

'How would you change things if you could? OK, you're the government, all of a sudden, you have the power, what would you do?'

'Er, I'd keep school down to one day a week . . . Or private lessons at home. Yeah. That's better.'

'OK.'

'OK. How about you, Claudia? Do you like school?'

'Most of the time no.'

'What do you dislike?'

'Er – teachers again. It's really the headmistress. She – she's useless.'

'In what way?'

'She just is. I don't know . . . explain it, can you? She just – she can't teach, . . . she can't do things, she's useless. She doesn't understand things.'

"Look – if you have five pocket calculators and I take two away, how many have you got left?"

"I often say, Mrs Dent, I'd rather have your little Christopher in my class than all the bright, clever ones!"

B Should children have more freedom?

1 Vocabulary revision. Put in words and expressions from the box (there are three too many).

actually	afraid	arguments	beliefs	boring	change	cheerful	death	department
ear-ring	find out	future	introduced	kind	machine	met	nonsense	part-time
problems	reason	refused	sky	slim	spare time	spends	strange	striped
suit	wearing	world	worth				

I .....1..... Simon at a party – it was my ex-boyfriend who .....2..... us, ...3..... He was .....4..... a really good .....5..... and a beautiful .....6..... shirt, with a very expensive-looking .....7..... in one ear, and I thought 'Now's your chance, girl – here's a boy with some money, for a .....8.....' In fact, he hasn't got a penny. Because, of course, he .....9..... it all on clothes. But he's a .....10.... sort of guy, and he's very good-looking – .....11..... and dark – and he's very .....12.... to me, so really I'm quite glad we met.

We both have .....13.... jobs, so we have a lot of .....14...., and we spend most of it together. We talk about a lot of things, and we have a lot of laughs, but I'm .....15.... we do have quite a lot of .....16.... too. One .....17.... for this is that he has so many .....18...., ...19.... He believes in life after .....20....; he thinks you can .....21.... about the .....22.... by reading horoscopes; he says he's seen spaceships up in the .....23....; he's got some crazy plan to build a time .....24..... He talks about all sorts of .....25.... like that, and I must say it gets on my nerves a bit. I think there are enough .....26..... in this .....27.... without inventing new ones. But I suppose it would be .....28.... if everybody was the same, wouldn't it?

2 Present perfect progressive. What do you think these people have been doing? Example:

A: *She's been playing tennis.*

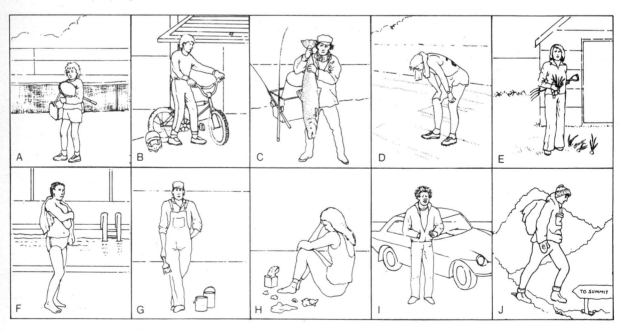

3 Grammar revision. Put in *can, can't, will, would, should, may* or *must*.

1. 'There's somebody at the door. Who .... it be?' 'It .... be Barbara – she's in Scotland.' 'Of course, it .... be Mike. He said he'd call in to collect his shopping.'
2. What .... you do if you lose your job?
3. What .... you do if you had to sell your house?
4. We haven't decided where to go on holiday. We .... go to Wales again, but I'm not sure if we .... afford it.
5. I .... write to Dick – I've owed him a letter for months.
6. Excuse me – .... you lend me your pen for a moment?
7. Everybody .... know how to do simple first aid.
8. He .... be drunk – I .... understand a word he says.

4 Are you fit to be a parent? What sort of parent are you (would you be)? Strict, soft-hearted, or somewhere between the two? Answer the questions and check your score.

1. You have just been for a healthy five-mile run. Your pulse is somewhere over 200 and you wonder whether you are going to live. As you step out of the shower, your child walks into the bathroom, waves a paper in your face, and starts telling you all about the wonderful story he/she has just written about a rabbit with pink ears. As you stand there, dripping wet and searching for your glasses, what do you say?
   a. Lovely, dear. What's the rabbit's name?
   b. Super, darling. But could you just wait until I've dried myself and got dressed?
   c. If you and your bloody rabbit don't get out of the bathroom right now you're both going down the toilet.

2. You have told your child, about seventeen times, to calm down and stop jumping on the living-room furniture. Your child climbs up on the window-ledge and breaks a window. You tell the child that he/she will have to put two weeks' pocket money towards the cost of the repair, and you say that he/she can't go into the living room again for three days. Is this punishment:
   a. too strict?
   b. not strict enough?
   c. just right?

3. Your child is generally pretty well-behaved, but when his/her best friend Pat comes to play he/she turns into a wild beast. One day, they steal some lipstick and draw pictures all over the kitchen walls. Do you:
   a. say that Pat can never come again?
   b. try to explain to both of them why this is a bad thing to do?
   c. make them clean off the lipstick as well as they can?

4. What do you think about physical punishment?
   a. It's all right to smack a child occasionally for something very serious.
   b. Children need to be smacked when they're naughty – it's much better than telling them off.
   c. It is always wrong to smack a child.

5. Your child refuses to eat anything except crisps and ice cream. Do you:
   a. let him/her live on crisps and ice cream?
   b. make the child eat up everything that is on his/her plate at mealtimes?
   c. let the child have crisps and ice cream if he/she eats a certain amount of other food?

6. Your child is playing in the middle of the kitchen floor. When you say that you need to clean the floor, the child kicks and screams and refuses to move. Do you:
   a. forcibly move the child and his/her toys?
   b. explain to the child why it is important that you clean the floor now?
   c. put off cleaning the floor till later?

7. At weekends, your child watches an average of eight hours' TV a day. He/she is developing square eyes. Do you:
   a. have a discussion with the child, explaining why he/she should watch less TV?
   b. ration the child to three hours a day?
   c. let the child watch what he/she wants?

8. Your child's room looks like a rubbish dump that has been hit by a bomb. Do you:
   a. leave the child to tidy up the room when he/she feels like it?
   b. ask the child to tidy up the room?
   c. tell the child to tidy up the room?

(See score table and comments after Exercise 7.)

5 Write what you think about one of the questions in Exercises 6 and 7 of Student's Book Lesson 15B.

6 Read this text twice. The first time, see how much you can understand without using a dictionary. The second time, use a dictionary if you want to.

First day at school

But I was still shy and half paralysed when in the presence of a crowd, and my first day at the new school made me the laughing stock of the classroom. I was sent to the blackboard to write my name and address; I knew my name and address, knew how to write it, knew how to spell it; but standing at the blackboard with the eyes of the many girls and boys looking at my back made me freeze inside and I was unable to write a single letter.

'Write your name,' the teacher called to me.

I lifted the white chalk to the blackboard and, as I was about to write my mind went blank, empty; I could not remember my name, not even the first letter. Somebody giggled and I stiffened.

'Just forget us and write your name and address,' the teacher coaxed.

An impulse to write would flash through me, but my hand would refuse to move. The children began to titter and I flushed hotly.

'Don't you know your name?' the teacher asked.

I looked at her and could not answer. The teacher rose and walked to my side, smiling at me to give me confidence. She placed her hand tenderly upon my shoulder.

'What's your name?' she asked.

'Richard.' I whispered.

'Richard what?'

'Richard Wright.'

'Spell it.'

I spelled my name in a wild rush of letters, trying desperately to redeem my paralysing shyness.

'Spell it slowly so I can hear it,' she directed me.

I did.

'Now can you write?'

'Yes, ma'am.'

'Then write it.'

Again I turned to the blackboard and lifted my hand to write, then I was blank and void within. I tried frantically to collect my senses but I could remember nothing. A sense of the girls and boys behind me filled me to the exclusion of everything. I realised how utterly I was failing and I grew weak and leaned my hot forehead against the cold blackboard. The room burst into a loud and prolonged laugh and my muscles froze.

'You may go to your seat,' the teacher said.

I sat and cursed myself. Why did I always appear so dumb when I was called to perform something in a crowd? I knew how to write as well as any pupil in the classroom, and no doubt I could read better than any of them, and I could talk fluently and expressively when I was sure of myself. Then why did strange faces make me freeze? I sat with my ears and neck burning, hearing the pupils whisper about me, hating myself, hating them.

(from *Black Boy* by Richard Wright)

(from *Lots of Love* and *The Facts of Love*, compiled by Nanette Newman)

7 Try the crossword.

ACROSS

1. Very surprised.
5. This crossword should take you at .... ten minutes.
9. I'm not afraid of .... In fact, I think they're charming little creatures.
10. If you're delayed, this is what you have to do.
12. There was fog at both London airports, so we .... at Manchester instead.
14. Somebody who buys and sells. Marco Polo's father was one.
15. Are you afraid of small creatures – for example mice .... spiders?
16. 'How much .... have you got?' 'Just one suitcase.'
18. That woman.
20. People spent years looking for a northern sea .... from the Atlantic to the Pacific.
22. Can I change dollars into .... here?

23. Are you .... this is the right way?
25. Aircraft furnishings should be .... of material that won't burn.
26. If you're embarrassed, your face may go ....
27. Happy New .... !

DOWN

1. I'd like to be .... to speak more languages.
2. Woman's name.
3. The airline decided to close up two of the .... exits so that they could fit in more seats.
4. How .... you sleep?
5. I've just had a .... from Andrew.
6. I'll be .... from the office all next week – I have to go to Belgium.
7. Unhappy.
8. Fix with string.
11. I dreamt last night that a .... fell on our house.
13. Animal kept as a pet, or used for hunting.
17. Try to .... going through the centre of Oxford – the traffic's terrible.
18. If I could take a couple of years off, I'd like to .... maths.
19. 'How long have you lived .... ?' 'Nearly two years.'
21. Air fares from Europe to the .... have got much cheaper.
24. Smoking .... non-smoking?

(*Solution on page 138.*)

ARE YOU FIT TO BE A PARENT?

1. a–3 b–2 c–1
2. a–3 b–2 c–1
3. a–1 b–2 c–3
4. a–2 b–1 c–3
5. a–3 b–1 c–2
6. a–1 b–2 c–3
7. a–2 b–1 c–3
8. a–3 b–2 c–1

TOTAL 8–13: You are (or would be) a pretty strict parent. Don't forget that children need patience, understanding and love as well as firmness.

TOTAL 14–19: You (would) try to be neither too strict nor too easy-going. This can be very good if children know what to expect; but it is no good being strict about something one day and soft about it the next.

TOTAL 20–24: You tend towards soft-heartedness. Be careful: children need some limits, so they can define themselves as people and set their own limits later on. The children will know that you love them if you set the limits in a firm but loving way.

Places

A Australia

1 Grammar revision: copy the text and put in suitable prepositions. Some can be used more than once; more than one answer is possible in some cases.

across	along	by	down	for	into	outside	over	past	round	through	to
towards	under	until									

Let me tell you how to get .....1..... our place. Are you coming .....2..... car? OK. You drive .....3..... the A1734 .....4..... Blackstone .....5..... about twelve miles; go .....6..... the first turn to Stroop, take the second turn, and then go straight on .....7..... you come to a crossroads. Go straight .....8..... the crossroads, ...9..... a petrol station, take the next right and drive .....10..... the park. On the other side of the park, go .....11..... the canal bridge, ...12..... the hill, turn left .....13..... the Market Square, keep straight on .....14..... the railway bridge and you'll come .....15..... Miller Street. It's probably best to park there, because there isn't usually a space .....16..... our house. We're just .....17..... the corner from the post office – 37 Jackdaw Lane.

2 Grammar revision. Make sentences from the table. Examples:

After I finish my exams I'm going to go to Australia.
Before I go to Australia I'm going to finish my exams.

FIRST	THEN	CONJUNCTION
finish exams	go to Australia	after/before
go for some job interviews	leave for Australia	before
interviews finished	catch next plane for Sydney	as soon as
arrive in Sydney	go straight to see old girlfriend	when
leave Sydney	look around New South Wales and Queensland	after
buy good car	go north	before
get to Northern Territory	need something with 4-wheel drive	when
get back from trip	sell car again	after
spend week surfing	leave Australia for good	before
get back from Australia	have to start new job	when

3 Read these two Australian aborigine poems.

White man got no Dreaming,
Him go 'nother way.
White man, him go different,
Him go road bilong himself.

No more boomerang
No more spear.
Now all civilised –
Colour bar and beer.

colour bar: discrimination against coloured people

4 Read this with a dictionary. (It is the transcript of the interview with Annemarie and Tony, Student's Book Lesson 16A, Exercises 3–5.)

(T = Tony; A = Annemarie; I = Interviewer)

T: I come from Sydney, which is – it's a beautiful place – if you've got to have a city, Sydney's probably the best place in the world to build one, because of the harbour and the light and the space.

I: If you had to live in Australia, what part of Australia would you live in?

A: I would live in Sydney, or near it, certainly . . . Oh, I think that's – that's the other thing about Australia. Because I really don't like living in big cities. And yet, if I had to live in Australia, I couldn't bear to live out in the country. Because it is so dead and so cut off from the world. Anywhere else you can live in the countryside and yet be very close to city culture, which I like. Whereas in Australia – probably on the east coast – probably near Sydney would be possible – but small towns in Australia are deadly – very very deadly – so I would live in Sydney.

* * * * *

I: How would you say that Australia feels different from England?

T: Physical space – would you?

A: Erm, yes.

T: First thing – light – quality of light – the quality of light's very harsh. It's physically a very harsh environment, isn't it? . . .

A: But parts of the coast – parts of the Australian coastline aren't so different to parts of the coastline around here.

T: Southern coast. New South Wales is very green and rolling.

A: Yes, no, it's the –

T: interior

A: interior that's very very different. Erm, it's very stark. The vegetation, the flora, is completely different – you don't get any similar trees and flowers.

T: (Simultaneously) It's desert flora, desert fauna – I mean it's animals that have survived – but they're not particularly spectacular. I think, because it's such a large area, er it varies considerably. We've got the Snowy Mountains, a range of mountains, which are cold, not very high, but there's snow, so there's skiing. Erm . . .

A: Yes, but that's a very small part of the whole country.

T: Yes, but you've got everything. You've got subtropical up north . . .

A: But because it's so big, you don't necessarily get to see it all, if you – even if you've lived there all your life . . . (Unclear) the Snowy Mountains until – you know, until I was in my twenties. A lot of people never get there at all, so they don't know what snow looks like, or high mountains.

T: No, I saw my first snow in Russia in 1972. So you're right. I mean, it is a big country. I've never been to Perth – I've been halfway round the world, in different forms of transport, but I've never been to Perth . . .

A: It's 3,000 miles.

T: . . . which is 3,000 miles away. And it's across the desert. It's across a very large, inhospitable desert, even though there's now a tarmacked highway that runs east-west across the country, the people in Perth still talk of the East Coast as another country, 'over there'.

A: Do they?

T: Oh, yeah, it's very peculiar, they talk about it as 'over th–'; everything else is 'over there'. Because Perth is the only thing – the only major city in one half of the continent, that's the same size as North America.

A: And the rest is desert.

T: Yes, it's desert. Well, it's not – yes, it is desert – it's very harsh country. And it's made the people harsh, in a way. It's made them very direct. Conversationally very direct. And conversationally minimal. I mean, they don't talk to one another, do they?

* * * * *

A: Yes, I didn't think it would bother me. It's beginning to bother me now.

T: The weather?

A: The long winter, and there's not enough sun.

T: Not enough sun.

A: But I couldn't go back and live in Australia just for the climate. People do.

T: People do. I've some Welsh friends who live in Sydney.

A: And they say that that's the only reason they're there. They'd be much happier in Wales. But they stay for the climate. I can't see that happening to me.

I: Are you able to – this would interest me to know – are either of you able to separate out – do you think it's the fact that it's cold and/or wet, or is it the light, is it the number of hours of light that bothers you?

A: Yes, I think it's the – the lack of sunshine. It's so beautiful when the sun is out.

T: It's too grey here. (Unclear) It's grey and damp.

I: I find the number of – for myself, the number of hours of sunshine in the winter is so small.

T: It's terrifying. You just get up and it's dark again.

* * * * *

T: Yes, the physical environment, the space, the physical space between people.

I: What do you mean?

T: Well, there's more – here, the physical space between people, even though here I think people are more inhibited about touching one another or the closeness, are very much more aware of personal space here than we are at home. And they tend to stand closer. I find people in Australia tend to stand further apart, and shout at one another. Because the physical space is there. The car parks there are like huge auditoriums, open-air auditoriums. There's space –

A: Do you like that?

▶

T: Yes. No. I know – Yes, I do like it. I mean, it can be – it can be vacant and deadly. But I noticed it in Russia as well. Physical space. And Russia more so, because the thing's – everything that is built is built big. People are big. Trains are bloody big. Everything's huge. As it is in Australia. And the space and the light. The light you get from a large horizon or a big sky is nice. Sometimes this drives me up the wall, Britain. Everything's like a small picture. You're in a small picture . . . Houses are – houses have space, they have room in the front and the back. Cars are bigger.

* * * * *

T: . . . and I was very unimpressed with Britain. There are still things here that I'm not very happy about.

I: Like what?

T: Well, the – the lack of push in people. I mean, pushiness is an Australian thing as much as it is an American thing, I mean, a desire to get out and get what you want, and I think, to see that you can get it. Australians still see that. Whether it's a myth now or not doesn't matter. But I think it affects the personality. It gives you confidence. Erm, it gives you desire. I see the lack of desire here as terrifying, sometimes in people. They've given up.

A: I don't find it quite as depressing as you do.

T: I don't find it so depressing. I see the difference. And the differences that I don't like are those. The differences that I do like, erm, er, I like living here. But there are fantastic differences between the British and the Australians.

5 Complete the text with words from the box.

> atmospheric   climate   coast   concerts   crowds   depressing   deserts   environment
> exactly   landscapes   physical   restaurants   sickness   space

She comes from Houston, Texas and I come from Oxford, England. I think Houston has a horrible ....1...... Being on the ....2.... of the Gulf of Mexico, it's both hot and humid, and there's bad ....3.... pollution from the oil refineries. She thinks Oxford is pretty ....4....: it's cold most of the year, there's no sun and it rains a lot. So we have more or less decided to live somewhere else. What we haven't decided yet is ....5.... where. Our ....6.... ....7.... is important to both of us, and we both love beautiful ....8..... I especially like mountains, and feel good at a high altitude; she gets altitude ....9.... if she goes upstairs. I like a cool damp climate; she doesn't like rain. She likes ....10....; I can't stand heat. We both need ....11...., and feel happy in wild areas a long way from civilisation; we also both like cinemas, theatres, art galleries, ...12.... and good food and wine. I hate big cities; she loves pavements and ....13...... Probably if we weren't together, I would live in North Wales and she would divide her time between Paris and Texas. However, we'd quite like to stay together, so we have this problem. Does anybody know a hot flat cool mountainous desert with no people, plenty of culture and some good ....14....?

6 What kind of places do you like? Write a few paragraphs, using as many words and expressions as you can from Exercise 5 above.

"Call me an old sentimental, mate, but when the old girl asks you for a fur coat, how can you refuse?"

B A beautiful place

1 Grammar: past perfect tense. Imagine that a forgetful old lady went out one evening to see some friends. She had a number of problems. Find reasons for them, using the past perfect tense. Example:

Why didn't she get to her friends' house?
Because she had forgotten their address.

1. Why didn't she look in her address book?
2. Why didn't she phone home and ask her daughter for their address?
3. Why didn't she go back home?
4. Why couldn't she get a hotel room?
5. Why did she get wet?
6. When she found her home, why couldn't she open the front door?
7. Why did her daughter take a long time to let her in?

2 Past perfect tense. Put together the following ideas to make sentences about a burglary. Use *although* or *because* + past perfect in each sentence. Example:

*We thought we might be burgled **because** our neighbours **had been burgled** the week before.*

1. we thought might be burgled – neighbours burgled week before
2. burgled last Saturday; burglar obviously knew we were out – we left lights on
3. he got in easily – we locked door
4. got in without making noise – we forgot to switch on burglar alarm
5. burglar didn't find jewels – we hid them
6. got money – we put in safe
7. found passports and credit cards – left in desk drawer
8. burglary very expensive for us – forgot to renew insurance

3 Vocabulary revision. Can you match the words and the shapes in each group?

circle   cube   curve   dotted line   oval   pyramid   rectangle   sphere   square
straight line   triangle

4 Vocabulary revision. Match the words and the numbers.

back   bottom   button   corner   edge   end   front   handle   knob   point   side
switch   top

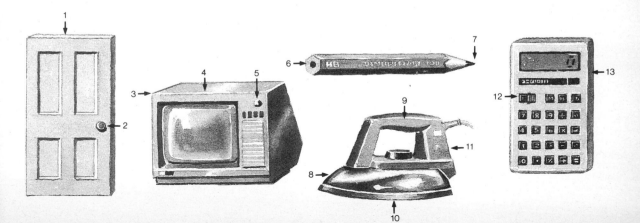

5 Pronunciation. Copy the words and underline the stressed syllables.

activity   atmosphere   cartoon   climate
committee   constructive   co-operative
critical   desert   enthusiastic   interior
landscape   mention   method   moderately
prepare   rectangular   teenager
upbringing   variety   vegetation

6 Fast reading test. Use a watch for this, and see how many answers you can write in 3 minutes.

1. If the pyramid is on the cube, write the opposite of *black*; otherwise write your name.

2. If the cube is higher than the sphere, write the letter that comes after *S* in the alphabet; otherwise write the letter that comes before *S*.

3. If a square has got less corners than a triangle, write the name of the day after Tuesday. Otherwise write the name of the month before October.

4. Write the name of the shape that is between the square and the circle.

5. Write the name of the shape that is between the cube and the triangle.

6. Write the name of the day before the day after the day before yesterday.

7. If a cube has not got more corners than a sphere, draw a straight line. Otherwise draw a curve.

8. If two pyramids have more corners than a cube, draw a square. Otherwise draw a circle.

9. Write the name of the day before the day after the day after tomorrow.

10. Write your name backwards or draw a pyramid upside down.

11. What time will it be this time tomorrow?

12. Draw a circle inside a rectangle inside a triangle inside a square.

7 EITHER: Write a description of a place that you like or dislike very much.
OR: Describe a place on earth as seen from the point of view of an explorer from another planet.

8 Read one or more of these poems.

STOPPING BY WOODS ON A SNOWY EVENING

Whose woods these are I think I know.
His house is in the village though;
He will not see me stopping here
To watch his woods fill up with snow.

My little horse must think it queer
To stop without a farmhouse near
Between the woods and frozen lake
The darkest evening of the year.

He gives his harness bells a shake
To ask if there is some mistake.
The only other sound's the sweep
Of easy wind and downy flake.

The woods are lovely, dark and deep,
But I have promises to keep,
And miles to go before I sleep,
And miles to go before I sleep.

(Robert Frost)

CURAÇAO

I think I am going to love it here.

I ask the man in the telegraph office
the way to the bank.
He locks the door and walks with me
insisting he needs the exercise.

When I ask the lady at my hotel desk
what bus to take to the beach
she gives me a lift with her beautiful sister
who is just driving by in a sports job.

And already I have thought of something
I want to ask the sister.

(Earle Birney)

COMING DOWN

Coming down from the summit
it was all different.
Suddenly the world was tame
and upside-down.
We began to talk about work
mortgages
children
wives.
Then, below the first ice-field
Bellini stopped, and said
'Next year
we do the East Face direct.'
We looked back
and everything was all right again.

(Lewis Mancha)

Getting things done

A Coffee, toothpaste and pencils

1 Grammar revision: passives. Put in the correct verb forms.

1. The palace .... by Sir Robert Fleming. (*build*)
2. It .... completely .... by fire in 1745. (*destroy*)
3. Seven years later, it .... as an exact copy of the original. (*rebuild*)
4. In the 18th century it had 48 rooms, but it .... in the late 19th century, and now has 112 rooms. (*enlarge*)
5. In 1976 it .... to Leisuredesign Enterprises Ltd. (*sell*)
6. The house .... into a fun palace, and the gardens .... into a safari park. (*convert, turn*)

2 Here are some of the notices in the fun palace and safari park. Can you fill in the gaps with passive verbs?

1. Visitors .... into the house and grounds between 9.00 am and 5.30 pm. (*allow*)
2. A bell .... fifteen minutes before closing time. (*ring*)
3. Visitors .... not to feed the animals. (*request*)
4. People .... not to leave their cars while touring the safari park. (*advise*)
5. Dogs .... in the safari park. (*not allow*)
6. You .... not to touch the furniture. (*ask*)
7. The staff .... to accept tips. (*not permit*)
8. Lunch .... in the cafeteria from 11.00 to 2.30. (*serve*)

3 This is a genuine news report, published in June 1986. Can you fill in the gaps with words from the box?

locked	rescued	trapped	were (twice)

In Denmark, 24 people .....1..... left hanging upside down when a roller coaster car made an unscheduled stop. The passengers were .....2..... 60 feet in the air for twenty minutes before they were .....3..... by firemen with ladders. An official for the fairground, at Aalborg in western Denmark, said the riders had been firmly .....4..... in and had not been in danger. 'They .....5..... given their money back,' the official said.

4 Spelling revision: double or single letters?
Write the past participles. Examples:

trap – trapped   wait – waited
forget – forgotten

stop   clean   end   slam   tin   start
help   beg   aid   chat

5 Write a paragraph to say how a musical
mousetrap is made, using the notes to help you.

– musical mousetraps made by specially trained
  craftsmen in central Fantasia
– olive wood imported from Redland
– left to stand in rain for three years
– when ready, cut and polished on special
  machines
– pieces carefully fixed together with silver screws
– small music boxes (measuring less than one cubic
  centimetre) made by craftsmen's wives
– designed to play either Chopin or jazz
  (depending on kind of mouse to be caught)
– music box fixed into floor of cage
– trap now ready to catch mice: mousetrap placed
  on floor near mousehole and music box wound
  up
– mice irresistibly attracted to music and caught

MARCIE GLICKMAN
85% PIZZA
15% PEPSI

6 Read this with a dictionary.

Work expands so as to fill the time available for its
completion. General recognition of this fact is shown in
the proverbial phrase 'It is the busiest man who has time
to spare'. Thus, an elderly lady of leisure can spend the
entire day in writing and dispatching a postcard to her
niece at Bognor Regis. An hour will be spent in finding the
postcard, another in hunting for spectacles, half an hour
in a search for the address, an hour and a quarter in
composition, and twenty minutes in deciding whether or
not to take an umbrella when going to the pillar box in the
next street. The total effort that would occupy a busy man
for three minutes may in this fashion leave another person
prostrate after a day of doubt, anxiety and toil.

(from *Parkinson's Law* by C. Northcote Parkinson)

"Have you any – 'Do It Herself' books?"

B Make it yourself

1 Vocabulary revision and extension. What are these things called, and what are they used for? Match the nouns, the verbs and the pictures. Example:

saucepan – boil – A

bowl   cloth   food processor   frying pan
grater   knife   mug   oven   saucepan
sink

boil   cut   drink   fry   grate   mix
prepare   roast/bake   wash up   wipe

2 Vocabulary revision and extension. Do you know what all these verbs mean? Match the words and the pictures.

bend   break   cut   hit   mend   scratch
slice   squeeze   turn   twist

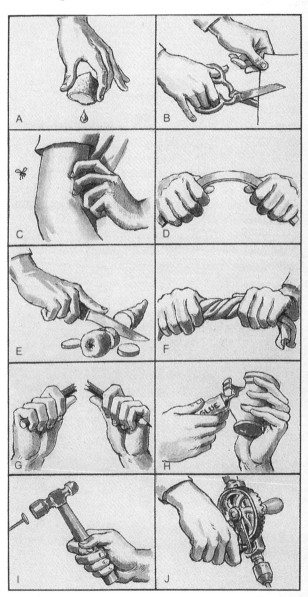

3 Vocabulary revision and extension. Match tools and instruments from the left-hand column with the descriptions of their uses from the right-hand column, and with the pictures. Use a dictionary if necessary. Then make sentences like the one in the example, to say what the tools/instruments are used for. Example:

A: *A screwdriver is a tool which is used to turn screws.*

TOOLS AND INSTRUMENTS	USES
axe	shape lengths of wood
barometer	turn screws
chisel	turn nuts
drill	hit nails
file	smooth wood
hammer	make holes
lathe	measure air pressure
microscope	cut down trees
plane	measure temperature
saw	cut pieces out of wood
screwdriver	cut lengths of wood
spanner	see distant things
telescope	see small things
thermometer	smooth metal

4 Grammar: passives (verbs with two objects). The table shows what various people were given for Christmas. Make passive sentences, using the structure *X was given . . .* Example:

Harry was given two pairs of gloves and a book.

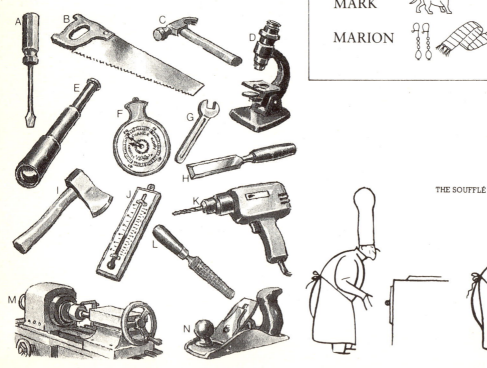

THE SOUFFLÉ

5 Read the text with a dictionary. Then write a few lines saying which suggestion you think is most useful, and why. Do you think any of the suggestions are useless? If so, why? Can you add any suggestions of your own?

TWENTY WAYS OF SAVING MONEY

1. Save money on holidays by exchanging homes with a foreign family.
2. Learn to do your own simple plumbing and electrical repairs.
3. Knit your own sweaters.
4. Drive smoothly, without sudden stops and starts – it uses less petrol.
5. Don't drive when you can walk.
6. Telephone people at times when you know they're busy – your conversations will be shorter.
7. Put your telephone in an uncomfortable noisy place.
8. Form a group with other people to share the shopping – you won't have to drive to the shops so often, and you'll save money by buying in bulk.
9. Invite people to tea or coffee instead of dinner.
10. Borrow books from the public library instead of buying them.
11. Buy fewer newspapers and magazines – you probably don't read them all anyway.
12. Don't use a dishwasher or washing machine without a full load.
13. Take showers instead of baths.
14. Buy cheap throwaway shoes for rough wear (expensive shoes need expensive mending).
15. Don't send sheets to the laundry – use non-iron sheets and wash them yourself.
16. Drink water instead of expensive soft drinks.
17. Be very careful about turning lights off when they are not needed.
18. If you have a garden, grow your own vegetables.
19. Make your own jam and marmalade.
20. Learn to do your own hair.

6 Write as many suggestions as possible for either saving water or saving electricity.

Unit 18

Needs

A People going hungry

1 Grammar revision. Make one sentence out of each pair.

1. I gave the money to a man. I can't see him. (Begin '*I can't . . .*')

   I can't see the man I gave the money to.

2. The money was in a box. The box is still here. (Begin '*The box . . .*')

   The box the money was in is still here.

3. Ethiopia gets aid from some countries. These countries are mainly in the northern hemisphere. (Begin '*The countries that Ethiopia . . .*')
4. Emergency food is carried in trucks. Some of them are very old. (Begin '*Some of the trucks . . .*')
5. I give money to some charities. I'm careful about which charities. (Begin '*I'm careful about . . .*')
6. She took the papers out of a file. I don't know which file. (Begin '*I don't know . . .*')
7. The Patels live on a small farm. It has been flooded three times in three years. (Begin '*The small farm the Patels . . .*')
8. War on Want puts its money into projects. The projects are designed to help poor women especially. (Begin '*The projects War . . .*')

2 Revision. Choose a word from the box to put into each blank, using some words more than once.

about	at	by	for	in
of	on	through	to	

1. That's very kind .... you.
2. Are you interested .... politics?
3. How can I find out .... things to do in the area?
4. I didn't know Adrian was married .... Gloria.
5. I only listen .... the radio when I'm in the car.
6. Do you believe .... God?
7. What was the reason .... the delay?
8. What do you think .... the US's latest move in the Middle East?
9. What time we get there will depend .... how bad the traffic is.
10. I sometimes dream .... having enough free time to travel all over Europe.
11. Unemployment in this area has risen .... 10% this year, because .... the factory closures.
12. Some birds, ... example the robin, stay in Britain all year round.
13. Going .... customs can take quite a while in America.
14. I really didn't do it .... purpose, but I know she thinks I did.
15. How did Marco Polo travel – .... land or .... sea?
16. Are you coming .... car or .... foot?
17. I'm really proud .... my mother, being so independent at her age.
18. Are you any good .... repairing cars?
19. We'll try to come earlier, but we'll be there .... eight o'clock at the latest.
20. What did you talk ....?

3 Use words from the box to fill blanks in the text. You may have to make plurals or change verb forms.

alive	control	emergency	flood	hunger	hungry
join	need (twice)	politics	poor	poverty	
project	public	surplus	world		

WAR ON WANT: GENERAL SECRETARY'S REPORT

It's been a bad year for .....1..... people. Cyclones, ...2...., civil wars – and above all famine – have cut into humanity, killing literally millions.

George Orwell said that the ultimate in obscenity would be reached when half of the people in the .....3..... could watch the other half starving to death on television. This year his prediction was realised. The world was stunned by the pictures. At times it seemed like a horrible dream, to watch children, families, whole communities dying of .....4..... in a world of plenty.

Yet if you boarded an aeroplane in England in the morning, you could stand as I did in the refugee camps on the Sudan-Ethiopia border before dark the same day. Which poses the question – if those .....5..... people can be reached by scheduled airline in less than one day – why is the situation still not under .....6.....?

The reasons are little to do with nature – and a lot to do with .....7.....

If a tiny fraction of the treasure which sent the Task Force to the Falklands had moved the European food .....8..... to the famine, it would by now have been stopped.

Even worse, if the simple message that 'a stitch in time saves nine' had been learnt, and relatively little had been spent on starting long-term development .....9..... ten years ago, the famine would never have occurred, millions would be .....10...., and the millions of pounds in .....11..... relief would never have been .....12..... But the political will in the developed world is not there.

But if the politicians have failed the people have not.

In the wave of .....13..... generosity, War on Want has this past year made its greatest ever contribution to the war on want in emergency aid, medium and long-term development, education, agitation and effective campaigning.

But the war has got tougher, the enemy – .....14..... – stronger, the casualties – the world's poor – more numerous.

We .....15..... to enlist more money, understanding, support and above all more people.

Come and .....16..... us – the War on Want is still the only war worth fighting in the world today.

George Galloway
General Secretary

4 Vocabulary revision and extension. Copy these two vocabulary networks and add as many words as you can to each of them.

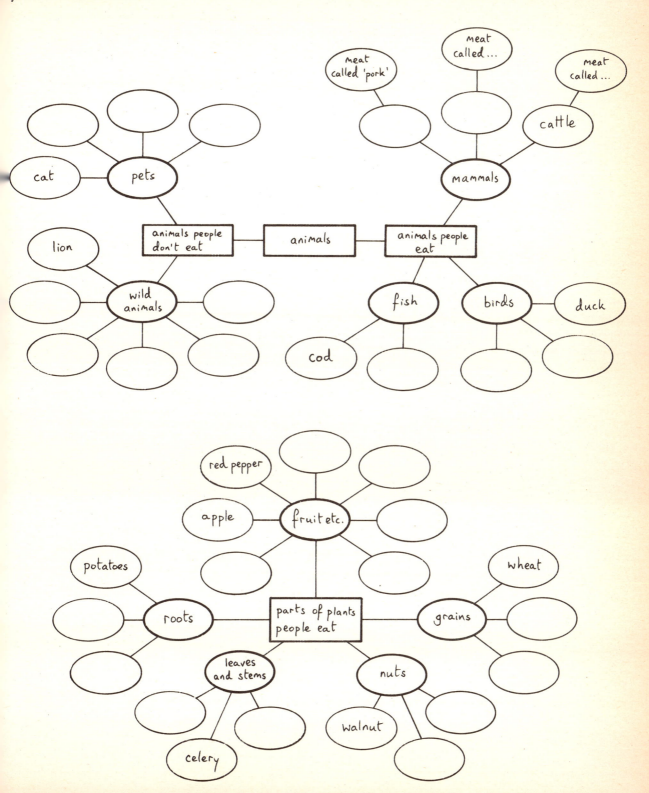

5 Make each pair of sentences into one sentence. Use words from the box to join the halves; you can take out some words and change the word order. In some cases more than one solution is possible.

although	as	as soon as
because	since	unless
until	when	while

1. We in Oxfam don't work through governments. We can work on both sides of a struggle in a circumstance like the civil war in Ethiopia.

2. We have field officers. They do not start projects, but wait for local people to come to them with ideas.

3. We don't have Oxfam people working on projects in the field. We don't believe that Westerners can come into other countries and tell people there what they need.

4. Britain is financing big projects like hydroelectric power stations in third world countries. People in these same countries are dying from the need for smaller projects like clean-water programmes.

5. Everyone in the world will have clean water one day. Up to that time, hundreds of thousands of babies will die every year.

6. 'Aid' from Britain often involves buying advice or goods from British firms. The 'aid' is really going to Britain!

7. The British people might demand that their politicians change the way aid is given. If not, nothing will ever change.

8. Oxfam gives poor people more control over their own lives. Immediately, they gain a sense of self-respect and work hard to succeed.

9. Sir Winston Churchill heard about Oxfam's being founded. He said it was unpatriotic.

6 Choose one of the two texts to read. When you read the first time, put a circle around the words you don't know but can guess the meaning of; put a line under the words you must look up to understand the text. Look up the underlined words in the dictionary and read the text again.

Good food dustbin guide

Two high school students from the Norwegian oil capital of Stavanger have recently completed a fortnight's holiday living out of other people's dustbins. They report that it was a very tasty gastronomic tour.

Torbjoern Groenning, 16, and Kolbjoern Opstad, 18, had planned to live as cheaply as possible. They travelled by bike with their fishing rods, intending to live off what they caught and wild berries, buying only strict essentials. They claim it was "just a coincidence" that led them to look into one of the dustbins by the roadside: "Before we went to fish for our supper on the first afternoon, we threw away some rubbish."

Inside the dustbin near Helleland, they discovered four eggs, half a packet of paprika-flavoured crisps, four ham sandwiches, a tin of mackerel, two litres of skimmed sour milk, three different cheeses, one kilo of strawberries and an unopened can of Californian fruit salad. They also found a tube of sausage meat, half a kilo of margarine, a jar of plum jam and several loaves of bread.

The boys decided to turn their holiday into an investigative dustbin crawl. Their journey at the height of the tourist season took them from Stavanger, on Norway's south-west coast, to Mandel, a resort 180 miles further south and their revelations have since shocked Norwegians into thinking about how much they waste.

On one occasion they discovered 20 freshly cooked crabs in a picnic site dustbin. They ate them with a fresh loaf and some mayonnaise found at the same spot. Budding experts on dustbin survival, they collected deposits on empty bottles to buy themselves fresh milk. And to celebrate their best haul of bottles, worth £2, they bought themselves soft drinks and cream cakes.

There was one recurring practical problem: the heat. Torbjoern explains: "We could feel the asphalt melting under our bikes. So we never touched food that was not well-wrapped. We preferred unopened things and submitted anything else to a strict smelling-test."

Torbjoern and Kolbjoern are now active members of an ecological pressure group, called The Future in Your Hands, which claims 7,000 members and personalities such as Thor Heyerdahl and Gunnar Myrdal on its advisory board. The boys are already planning next year's holiday. They are considering a dustbin tour of Europe – to find out how much other holiday-makers throw away.
Alex Finer

(The Sunday Times)

When even the price of fasting is too high

Sir, – There must be many people who, in the face of the rapidly increasing cost of feeding a family, are considering giving up eating. We find ourselves thinking about it again exactly 12 months after last doing so, and have discovered an interesting fact or two which might be of help to others in the same situation.

Twelve months ago we estimated that the cost of two bottles of Perrier water per day – essential to the maintenance of health during fasting – would have cost us, at 30p per bottle, a total of £29.40 for a seven-day fast for us and our five children. Our take-home pay was then £42.57 and we decided that it was not an economical proposition.

The same seven-day fast would now cost us £47.04 out of our take-home pay of £47.84, and it is quite obvious that fasting has priced itself out of our range. These figures are based on the prices of Perrier water at our local branch of Sainsbury's.

We do, of course, have child benefit which has just been increased from £4 to £4.75 per child. The cost of a child's fasting for a week is £6.72, so we would need a further increase of £2 a week just to keep level with the cost of not eating. – Yours sincerely,
(Mrs) J. McGregor-Davies.
Cook's Wharf,
Rochester, Kent.

(The Guardian)

B In a bit of a panic

1 **What would you say in the following situations?**

1. Someone says, 'Oh, thank you very much!'
2. Someone phones for a chat just as you are about to leave to catch a train.
3. A good friend wants to borrow your car, but you are not insured for other people driving it.
4. You want to borrow a good friend's road map of England for a few days (you know he or she will not be needing it).
5. A friend asks to borrow your cassette recorder for the evening. You are happy to lend it to her.

2 **Make one sentence beginning 'Before . . . ' for each situation.**

1. Al is going to go shopping. He is going to put some petrol in the car first.
2. Virginia will telephone her mother. Then she will write to her brother.
3. Felicity will take the children to the birthday party. She will check on the exact address first.
4. I'll take my coat to the cleaner's. Then I'll come round to your place.
5. John will finish washing the car. Then the children will come home.

3 **Grammar revision. Use some of the words in the box to complete the sentences. In some cases more than one word may be correct.**

although	as	as soon as	because
since	unless	until	when	while

1. .... I don't really approve of all these charities, I always give something when they come to the door.
2. Well, I agree; I think the money should come from the government, but .... it doesn't, and the need is there, I always give a bit.
3. Things won't change .... government aid is spent more sensibly.
4. The ruler of some country that was receiving aid spent about £2 million on a state wedding .... the rest of the people were starving.
5. I don't give anything .... I know that a fair percentage of the money actually gets overseas.
6. Well, I gave to Band Aid, ... I think the money actually went direct to the cause.

4 **Pronunciation. Copy the words and underline the stressed syllables.**

capital   champagne   charity   damage
employee   forgive   individual   poverty
precious   process   remove   screwdriver
situation   thoroughly

5 **The sentences in this letter are out of order. Rewrite the letter, putting the sentences into a logical order.**

28 March

Dear Marilyn,

I think you mentioned that you had someone to look after your kids, and I thought she might include Helen. Please don't hesitate to say no if this presents any sort of problem. I won't actually be working most of the time – just giving one talk on each of the first three days, and a half-day session on the last morning. Love to Jerome and the kids – even if you can't fit Helen in, I hope we can see something of one another when I'm in Nice. I'm writing to ask you a favour. Would there be any possibility of her fitting in with your child care arrangements? I have to come to Nice from the 7th to the 10th of May for my work. Of course I would pay her extra for this. I thought it would be nice to bring little Helen along with me; but of course I have to make some arrangement for her to be looked after while I'm working.

Love,

Alex

6 **Now write a letter for one of these situations.**

1. Imagine the letter in Exercise 5 was written to you instead of Marilyn. The woman who looks after your children has made it clear that she doesn't want to look after any others. Suggest another solution, or say you'll try to find someone and write again soon.

2. You (and your family, or partner) would like to spend a couple of weeks in Wales. Your friend Jeremy has a flat there, and he has said in the past that you are welcome to use it. Write giving specific dates and asking if you can stay.

7 Grammar revision. Read the first dialogue and the account of it. Note the words and expressions in *italics* and how they correspond to the dialogue. Then read the second dialogue and write an account of it.

K: Oh, hello, Pat.

P: Hi, Kate, how's the baby?

K: Just great, thanks. Would you like a cup of tea?

P: No thanks, no time. But could you lend me your sewing machine for an hour or two?

K: Sure, glad to. Don't forget that the pedal sticks sometimes.

P: I won't. Shall I bring it back when I've finished?

K: No, just bring it to school this afternoon and I'll get it from you there.

P: OK. Thanks a lot, Kate.

K: Don't mention it. Bye.

P: Bye.

Kate and Pat *greeted one another* and Pat asked how Kate's baby was. Kate said she was great, and *offered* Pat a cup of tea. Pat said she didn't have the time and *asked Kate to* lend her her sewing machine for an hour or two. Kate *agreed*, and *told Pat not to* forget that the pedal stuck sometimes. Kate said she wouldn't, and asked if she should bring it back when she had finished. Kate *told her to* bring it to school that afternoon and she would get it from her there. Pat *thanked* her and they *said goodbye*.

J: Oh, hello, Bill, how are you?

B: Fine, Jim. Listen, could you lend me your food processor for a couple of hours? Mine has stopped working.

J: Sure. Do you know how to work this one? Is yours the same make?

B: Let's see, no, it isn't. Could you give me a demonstration?

J: Sure, just sit down. I'll make some breadcrumbs, I need them for tonight. Or why don't you make them?

B: OK, what do I do first?

J: Put the bowl on and turn it until it clicks. Yeah, then put the blade in and push it down.

B: Does it matter which way I put it in?

J: No, just put it in any way. But don't forget to push it down until it clicks.

B: Now what?

J: Cut the bread into squares – about six squares per slice, and put them in. OK, now put the top on with the tube to the left of the front, and then turn it to the right to start it.

B: Well, that's easy enough. Mine is much more complicated.

J: Yeah, well, I don't think you'll have any problems. Do you think you could bring it back when you've finished with it?

B: Sure, don't worry. I'll have it back by eight, if that's OK.

J: Fine. See you then. Bye, Bill.

B: Bye, Jim, and thanks a lot.

"I hope you don't mind me saying so, but it's been a pleasure to watch you eat."

"That's our problem, Charlie – the more we get, the more we want."

8 Try the crossword.

4. The feeling of not having eaten enough.
5. The opposite of *isn't*.
6. The developing countries (*two words*).
7. Like very small thin nails.
9. Half 15 across.
10. The noise of an explosion.
16. 'I don't understand.' '........... do I.'
18. Connect.
19. 'Anything else?' 'No, that's ...., thank you.'
21. You use it to see with.
22. Doctors .... patients.
23. *On* backwards is the opposite of this.
26. The past of *eat*.
28. A drink.
29. Painting, sculpture etc.
31. I'll let you know .... soon .... I can.
32. The opposite of the opposite of *on* backwards.

(*Solution on page 138.*)

ACROSS

1. Somebody who is employed.
4. The past of *hit*.
7. The opposite of *pull*.
8. A preposition.
10. You put rubbish in it.
11. .... people can afford to buy what they want.
12. An emotion which may lead to violence.
13. If you break the law you may have to .... to prison.
14. The past perfect progressive is a ....
15. Twice 9 down.
17. Not cooked.
20. A large proportion of the world's population live in ....
24. This person will tell you that black is white.
25. True, genuine, not imaginary.
27. If you borrow money from a bank you have to pay this.
30. Do you think dustmen should .... more than nurses?
33. Oxfam is one.
34. The opposite of *start*.

DOWN

1. Not too little; not too much.
2. .... people can't afford to buy what they need.
3. Rich person's boat.

...THIRD WORLD? I thought I had made only ONE!

Relationships

A They love each other a lot

1 Grammar revision: quantifiers with and without *of*. Choose suitable expressions from the box to complete the text. More than one answer is possible in some cases.

any (of)	each (of)	every	every one of
more (of)	most (of)	neither (of)	no
none (of)	several (of)	some (of)	

I've got two daughters; ....1.... them is married. My younger daughter, Ann, has had ....2.... boyfriends already than I've had in my whole life. I'm quite envious. She's got ....3.... boyfriends at the moment. I don't know how she does it, but she somehow manages to give ....4.... the boys the impression that he's the only one. I don't think ....5.... them knows about the others. ....6.... her boyfriends are very good-looking. But I don't think ....7.... boy who goes out with Ann can be very bright.

My other daughter is quite different – much more the faithful type. She's had ....8.... boyfriends, but always one at a time. And ....9.... relationship is very serious while it lasts. The two girls have quite a lot of arguments, of course. The older one always says that you need complete trust and honesty for ....10.... real relationship. Her sister says that ....11.... relationship is perfect all the time, so you might as well have a lot and get something different out of ....12.... them. ....13.... people criticise my younger daughter and say that her sister is right, but I'm not so sure. I think ....14.... her ideas are quite interesting, and if I was her age again I might behave in the same way.

2 Grammar revision: relative clauses. Choose five or more of the adjectives and make sentences to explain what they mean. Use the structure *A ... person is somebody who ...* Examples:

A bright person is somebody who thinks quickly.
A shy person is somebody who is afraid of contact with other people.

affectionate   argumentative   bright   dull
faithful   friendly   homosexual   honest
humorous   moody   shy   sociable   tolerant

3 Grammar revision: irregular verbs. Write the infinitive, past and participle of each of these verbs.

INFINITIVE	PAST	PARTICIPLE
bite	....	....
....	blew	....
....	....	frozen
hang	....	....
....	held	....
....	....	led
rise	....	....
....	sold	....
....	....	shaken
shine	....	....
....	showed	....
....	....	sung
spend	....	....
....	stole	....
....	....	stuck
swim	....	....
....	tore	....
....	....	thrown
wake	....	....
....	wore	....
....	....	won
wind	....	....

4 Write a few paragraphs about a relationship between two people that you know well. Use plenty of words and expressions from the lesson.

5 Read some or all of the following. Use a dictionary if necessary.

SMALL CHILDREN'S IDEAS ABOUT LOVE

my aunty falls in love when we go on holiday but she never likes it and she cries

I saw a book once with all drawings in it about falling in love and I think you have to have eggs.

It is silly to get Married before You are 12

I know what Love is, its the stuff they sell on the telly

I once saw some one fall in love In a car. It wasn't going though.

I sometimes think I love every thing and E verybody But I know I don't.

Me Dad went to prison and we have to keep remembring to love him

If you dont want to have a baby you have to wear a safety belt

kittens

You must take care of Love — if You Don't it goes bad

I saw my sister fall out of love it was very interesting

My cat falls in love and stays out all night and then he brings a lot of kittens back

(from *God Bless Love*, *Lots of Love* and *Vote for Love*, compiled by Nanette Newman)

93

B I'm shy of girls

1 Vocabulary revision and extension. Do you know the names of all the articles of clothing in the picture? Can you write the names of ten more articles of clothing?

2 Grammar revision: position of frequency adverbs. Use the adverbs from the box to say how often you do some of these things. Put the adverb in the right place (before the verb). Example:

I often write to my parents.

always	very often	often	quite often
sometimes	occasionally	hardly ever	
never			

How often do you:
– write to your mother/father/son/daughter?
– write to your brother/sister?
– buy flowers for people?
– start conversations with strangers?
– talk about your deepest feelings?
– lose your temper?
– kiss people?
– get attracted to people?
– fall in love?
– get depressed?
– cry?
– say 'I love you'?
– mean it?

3 Position of frequency adverbs (continued). Use the same adverbs to say how often you have done some of these things. Put the adverb after the first auxiliary verb. Examples:

I have often wished I could be alone.
I have never been hurt by somebody I loved.

How often have you:
– fallen in love with the wrong person?
– deliberately ended a relationship?
– been unhappy in a relationship?
– been happy in a relationship?
– wanted more friends?
– wanted fewer friends?
– wished you could be completely alone?
– been unpleasant to somebody you loved?
– been badly hurt by somebody you loved?

4 Read the letters. Which letter does each of the following sentences summarise best, in your opinion?

1. I live in a terrible world and nobody really understands my problems.
2. It's not their business.
3. What am I doing here?
4. Should I behave like everybody else?
5. Our attitudes are very different.
6. He's not good for her.
7. I don't believe her promises.

FALLING TO PIECES

My family seem to be falling to pieces. My parents argue over the silliest things. I'm sure they'll split up soon. And my four brothers really go on at me because I haven't got a job and have to keep borrowing money from Mum. But I never have any luck with jobs. I feel so lonely, I spend all my time just sitting at home.

Rich, London

I WANT TO GO HOME

I've been living in Italy for the past two years because of my husband's job. As far as he's concerned we're here for good. He's very happy and so are our children. But I can't seem to settle down. I just wait for each day to pass so that the time when we might move back to England comes nearer. Will things get better?

J.L., Rome

RUDE QUESTION

I am a 58-year-old accountant. I had a couple of heart attacks in the past, but I've had no problems for several years. I do a lot of sport and keep very fit. My weight hasn't changed since I was 20.

My problem is people who say, 'By the way, Joe, how old are you?' The question never has anything to do with our conversation. I don't care how old they are, so why should they worry about my age? I would like to tell them it's none of their business. Is there a tactful way to say it?

Joe, Edinburgh

SHE MUST END IT

Some weeks ago my sister-in-law told me she was having an affair. My brother has his faults, but I love him. She and I are also very close. I told her she must end the relationship. The man is married with a loving wife and three wonderful children.

She promised it would stop but it is still going on. She even had a weekend away with him – thanks to my covering up – so that she could finish the affair. But it seems they just had a great time together instead.

What should I do to end this situation before someone is hurt?

C.C., London

WILL HE BE FAITHFUL?

My lover and I are in our early forties and we are both divorced. We intend to get married but I'm not sure that he'll be a faithful husband.

As well as his ex-wife, he has two other women friends whom he sees quite often. When I object, he says his friends are not my business and he'll keep on seeing them when we're married.

I have one or two men friends, who he says are no concern of his, but I plan to give them up if we get married. And that's the difference between us.

Should we get married?

Rosemary, Cambridge

WHAT'S WRONG WITH ME?

All my friends say they've had sex with boys, but I haven't. They keep saying there's something wrong with me. If there is, can you tell me what it is and what I can do about it? I've been out with plenty of boys but I just haven't wanted to have sex.

J.D., Norwich

SHOULD I TELL MY FATHER?

Some time ago my father went to live with another woman. But my parents are still good friends and my father is very good about looking after us.

A few months ago my mother met another man. I was glad at the time because she was very lonely. Now I don't think it was quite such a good idea. He has a horrible temper and the other night he actually hit my mother. She begged me not to tell my father, which I wanted to do.

She refuses to give the man up and says I don't understand, even though I'm 14. She must be really lonely to want to go out with such a pig. I know my father is still fond of her and I think that if he knew what was happening he might even come back. Do you think I should disobey her and tell him?

Becky, Chester

5 Choose one of the letters and write an answer. Use some of these words and expressions.

Why don't you . . . ?
Why not . . . ? (e.g. *Why not try to forget him?*)
What/How about . . . ing?
I think you should . . .
You could/might . . .

If I were you, I would . . .
A good way to . . . is to . . .
The best way to . . . is to . . .
I think it's a mistake to . . .
Stop . . . ing and start . . . ing.

"It's just natural, that's all! We love you because you're ours, like the car."

"Your wife rang me to remind you to send me out for her birthday present from you."

"Did you ever pay that marriage bureau?"

THERE IS NO PRACTICE BOOK WORK FOR UNIT 20

Unit 21

Somewhere to live

A A lot needs doing to it

1 Look at the picture and write at least five things that need doing. Use the verbs in the box. Example:

His shoes need mending.

| clean   cut   mend   polish   press |
| sew on   wash |

96

2 Look at the illustration. It shows two memo lists – one written by a rich and lazy person, who does nothing for herself, the other written by a poorer person, who does everything for herself. Write a list of things that you must remember to do or to have done during the next week or so.

have hair cut
have nails manicured
have car polished
have eyes tested
have TV repaired
have suit cleaned
have bathroom
tap replaced
have cats brushed
have meat delivered
have party invitations
sent out

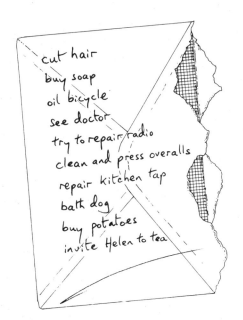

cut hair
buy soap
oil bicycle
see doctor
try to repair radio
clean and press overalls
repair kitchen tap
bath dog
buy potatoes
invite Helen to tea

3 Grammar revision. Complete the sentences with the prepositions from the box.

at	behind	by	in front of	inside	off
on	out of	over	through	under	

1. 'Could I use your phone?' 'Yes, it's over there .... the window.'
2. I think that picture would look better .... the fireplace.
3. How did those black marks get .... the ceiling?
4. I've just found your address book. It was .... your chair.
5. Could you tell the children to get their toys .... my bed and come .... my bedroom?
6. When we redecorated the living room we found an old cupboard .... the plaster.
7. It's colder .... this house than outside.
8. The windows are so dirty you can't see .... them.
9. If everybody will sit down .... the table, we can start eating.
10. That boy spends at least six hours a day .... the TV.

4 Spelling. Put the missing letters in the right places.

E, e, e, e, g, i, i, i, i, i, i, o, o, u, u, u, u, u, y

m–n–te
w–m–n
fr––nd
––rope
b–c–cle
for–––n
j––ce
bisc––t
m––stache

5 Read the text, using a dictionary only when really necessary, and then answer the questions in Exercise 6.

THE DAY THE CEILING CAUGHT FIRE

I never did like polystyrene ceiling tiles. Quite apart from the fire hazard, they don't look very good. So when I moved into a house whose previous owner had covered every ceiling with polystyrene tiles, I fully intended to take the lot down. I really did. It was just that there always seemed to be other things to do that were more urgent.

Now I can tell you that nothing is more urgent. If you have such tiles on your ceiling, take them down now. Tomorrow may be too late.

For that's the other thing about polystyrene tiles. They can turn a small fire into a killer. On the whole, we can congratulate ourselves on a very lucky escape.

Saturday, May 17, began as a fairly ordinary day. I got up at about 7 o'clock, took my wife Jean a cup of tea in bed, then set off for the south coast on business.

Jean rose shortly afterwards, did a few domestic chores, then left the house to make one or two family calls.

It was just as well that she did, for within an hour the house was filled with lethal black smoke and fumes. Burning plastic dripped from the ceiling, starting little fires in carpets or furniture.

A neighbour spotted the smoke pouring out of the shattered dining room window and called the fire brigade. Another neighbour managed to locate Jean, and she and the firemen arrived more or less simultaneously.

This was another piece of good luck, because it meant that they didn't have to break down a door to get in. Once inside, they put out the flames in what seemed a remarkably short time and without a mess; in fact, the only evidence that the fire brigade had been inside the house was that the fire was out.

They also called the electricity and gas boards, who sent representatives to check the safety of their respective installations. 'The wiring's all right – must have been a gas leak,' said the man from the electricity board. 'Nothing wrong with the gas – must have been an electrical fault,' said the gas man. Both were right, in a way. The trouble seems to have started in the electrical wiring of the cooker clock.

One thing is certain: without those ceiling tiles, it would have been a very localised fire, and might even have gone out by itself. As it was, the fire spread from the kitchen to the adjoining dining room. The heat shattered seven panes of glass, and charred one window frame so badly that it had to be replaced.

Two elderly armchairs in the dining room were destroyed, but the sofa escaped, as did the dining table. The fire brigade put out the flames before they reached the hall and stairwell, or it might have been a much more serious matter.

But the smoke damage . . .

Everything in the house was covered with an oily black film, almost impossible to remove. Every single item of clothing and bedding in the house needed to be washed, even those in drawers and cupboards.

There seemed to be nowhere the smoke hadn't penetrated. Everything we owned had to be sorted out into one of three categories: ruined, cleanable, or useable immediately (well, more or less). All the goods in category two – by far the largest – we bundled into a spare bedroom, and we're still working our way through the contents.

The insurance company paid up, with no more than the ordinary delay, for the damage to the house and the interior decoration. The ceilings have been covered with an ornamental plaster which has approved fire resistant qualities.

Now, four months later, things are slowly returning to normal. We feel we can invite people into our home again. But nothing can make us forget that we had a very lucky escape. The fire could have started at any time. Had it broken out during the night we would undoubtedly have been killed by the fumes long before anyone raised the alarm.

The discovery that you aren't fireproof is a very frightening one.

(from *Property Mover* – adapted)

" . . . Of course, it needs a lot doing to it."

6 Read the following sentences and decide whether they are true or false, according to the text in Exercise 5. Write *T* or *F*.

1. Polystyrene tiles are dangerous.
2. The author and his wife realise they were wrong to put them on the kitchen ceiling.
3. One day when they were both out a fire broke out.
4. It started with a gas leak in the cooker.
5. A neighbour saw flames coming out of the kitchen window and called the fire brigade.
6. Another neighbour told Jean that her house was on fire.
7. Luckily she had left the door unlocked, so the firemen didn't have to break it down.
8. The fire brigade didn't make a mess.
9. Two chairs in the dining room escaped.
10. But the dining room table was badly damaged.
11. Most of their possessions were ruined by smoke.
12. They were lucky the fire didn't start at night.

7 Write a short description of the house you are living in at the moment. Say what changes you would like to make.

"The whole place needs redecorating."

B More houses should be built

1 Vocabulary. Look at the example and then answer one or more of the questions, using as many of the words and expressions in the box as possible.

> turn . . . into . . .
> add   lengthen   remove   shorten
> straighten   strengthen   widen
> make . . . smaller/bigger/fatter

Example:
Suppose you wanted to turn a giraffe into a fox –
what would you have to do?
You would have to make the body much smaller;
shorten the neck; shorten the legs; lengthen the
tail; lengthen the nose; add more hair; change the
animal's colour; and make a number of other
changes.

What would you have to do if you wanted to:
1. change a rabbit into an elephant?
2. change a cow into a blackbird?
3. change a pig into a horse?
4. change a chicken into a lion?
5. change a shark into a butterfly?
6. change another creature (you choose) into something else?

2 Vocabulary revision and extension. Put some or all of the following words into groups (for example, *bank*, *interest* and *mortgage* could be put together). Add more words to some of the groups if you like.

air conditioning   bank   bath   brick
brush   build   buy   ceiling   cement
central heating   decorate   door
electricity   floor   fridge   gas   insurance
interest   kitchen   landlord   living room
mortgage   owner   paint   plaster   rent
repair   tenant   tiles   water   window pane

3 Grammar: passives. Complete these sentences with *should, ought to, may, might, can, could, will, would* or *must* + passive infinitive. (More than one answer may be possible.)

1. At least 500,000 more houses (*build*) as soon as possible.
   At least 500,000 more houses ought to be built as soon as possible.
2. But it is very unlikely that this actually (*do*).
   But it is very unlikely that this will actually be done.
3. Rents (*control*) by the government.
4. If that happened, the cost of living (*reduce*) by half.
5. We're afraid that our rent (*raise*) soon.
6. If we're unlucky, it (*double*).
7. Landlords (*prevent*) from putting up rents like that.
8. Mrs Anderson has promised to control rents if she becomes President, but I don't think she (*elect*).
9. And I don't think the present government (*expect*) to do anything about it.

4 Pronunciation. Copy the words and underline the stressed syllables.

accommodation   confuse   description
divorce   entertain   handicapped   illegal
improvement   interrupt   landlord
particular   structure   tenant

5 Write one or more paragraphs about the housing situation in your country.

6 Read the *Shelter* poster with a dictionary.

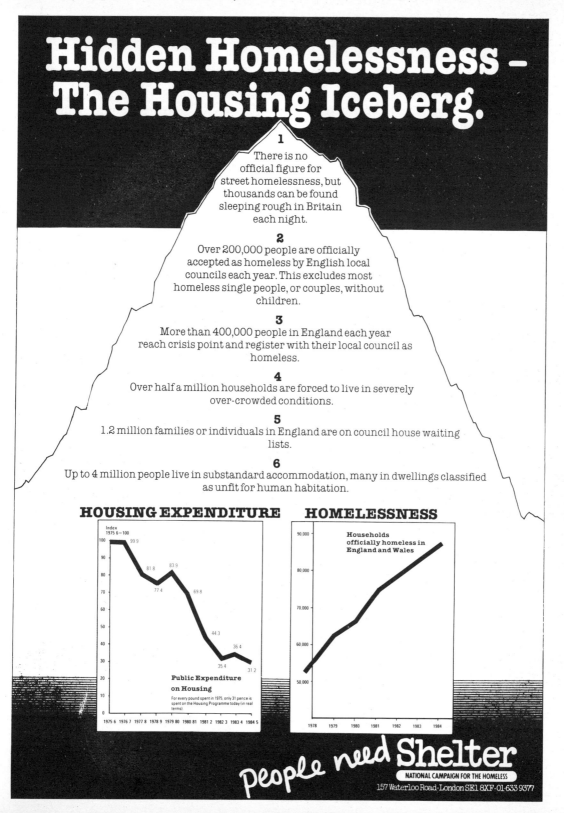

Hidden Homelessness – The Housing Iceberg.

1 There is no official figure for street homelessness, but thousands can be found sleeping rough in Britain each night.

2 Over 200,000 people are officially accepted as homeless by English local councils each year. This excludes most homeless single people, or couples, without children.

3 More than 400,000 people in England each year reach crisis point and register with their local council as homeless.

4 Over half a million households are forced to live in severely over-crowded conditions.

5 1.2 million families or individuals in England are on council house waiting lists.

6 Up to 4 million people live in substandard accommodation, many in dwellings classified as unfit for human habitation.

HOUSING EXPENDITURE

Index 1975 6 = 100

Public Expenditure on Housing

For every pound spent in 1975, only 31 pence is spent on the Housing Programme today (in real terms)

HOMELESSNESS

Households officially homeless in England and Wales

people need **Shelter**

NATIONAL CAMPAIGN FOR THE HOMELESS

157 Waterloo Road · London SE1 8XF · 01-633 9377

Describing people

A What do they look like?

1 Grammar. What is the difference between *so* and *such*? Look at the examples and then choose the best rule. Check the answer on page 138. Examples:

I'm so tired.
I've got such a headache.
I've got such a bad headache.
My headache's so bad.

Rule 1: *such* is more emphatic than *so*.
Rule 2: *such* is used before nouns; *so* is used before adjectives.
Rule 3: *such* is used before a noun, or before adjective + noun. *So* is used before an adjective without a noun.
Rule 4: *such* is used after *to have*; *so* is used after *to be*.
Rule 5: the difference is a question of style.

2 Put in *such* or *so*.

1. I'm .... handsome.
2. And I'm .... intelligent.
3. I've got .... a sense of humour.
4. And .... interesting ideas.
5. I'm .... a brilliant dancer.
6. And .... superior in every way.
7. It's really .... a pleasure to be with me.
8. I can't understand why I have .... trouble keeping my girlfriends.

3 Put in *so much, so many, so few* or *so little*.

When I agreed to serve on the committee, I didn't realise there would be .....1..... meetings – they take up .....2..... of my time that I think I'm going to have to resign. The meetings are completely useless anyway – people put .....3..... energy into arguing for hours and hours about things that have .....4..... importance that they weren't worth discussing in the first place. And .....5..... of the committee members are actually the kind of people I really want to get to know. I'm sure I'll be .....6..... happier if I give it up.

4 Grammar revision: modification of *too* and comparatives. Use expressions from the table to describe some of your features and parts of your body (or somebody else's). You can add other adjectives if you like. Examples:

*My eyes are possibly **a little too small**.*
*I wish my nose was **a bit shorter**.*
*It would be nice if my feet were **rather narrower**.*
*My mouth is **just right**.*

a bit	longer
a little	shorter
a fraction	wider
rather	narrower
a lot	bigger
much	smaller
far	etc.
	too long
	too short
	too wide
	etc.
just right	

"Gerald, do you remember how I used to say your head was shaped like an onion?"

5 Pronunciation. Practise saying these words with the correct stress.

at**tract**ive   **busi**nesswoman   **cheek**bones   de**scrip**tion   **eye**brows   **me**dium   mous**tache**
muscular   **over**weight

6 Read the descriptions, and then write a paragraph saying which of the people you would most or least like to meet, and why.

LILY SMALLS

(*She is looking in the mirror and talking to herself.*)
Oh, there's a face. Where you get that hair from? Got it from old tom cat. Give it back, then, love. Oh, there's a perm. Where you get that nose from, Lily? Got it from my father, silly. You've got it on upside down. Oh, there's a conk. Look at your complexion. No, you look. Needs a bit of make-up. Needs a veil. Oh, there's glamour. Where you get that smile, Lil? Never you mind, girl. Nobody loves you. That's what you think. Who is it loves you? Shan't tell.

(from *Under Milk Wood* by Dylan Thomas)

THE TRANSLATOR

The woman is watching me. She smiles sympathetically then goes back to her work. She is reading through a stack of foreign newspapers and occasionally marking an item with a thick black pencil. She is a linguist, fluent in most European languages. During the night the marked passages will be translated and Fidel will read them with his breakfast. She is not attractive. Her face is dominated by a large forehead and nose. Her neck is short and her shoulders box-like. But she is very intelligent. I wonder if she would trade her intelligence for beauty. But naturally. Stupid people never realise their stupidity. Beautiful people enjoy their attraction every waking moment. But the ultimate is to be beautiful and intelligent.

(from *Siege of Silence* by A.J. Quinnell)

BOOKREST

The girl lay back on the slope of the river bank, her eyes closed against the sun. Her dark hair fanned out on each side of her face, her white, even teeth biting on a long stalk of grass as the young man looked down at her. Her skin was pale despite the freckles on her neat, pert nose, but her mouth was poppy red, full and tempting.

The young man's hair was almost white and it lifted softly in the breeze off the river. He was reading silently from an open book that was resting on the girl's stomach.

(from *Codeword Cromwell* by Ted Allbeury)

PREHISTORIC WOMAN

She was just over four and a half feet (*1m 37*) tall, large boned, stocky, and bow-legged, but walked upright on strong muscular legs and flat bare feet. Her arms, long in proportion to her body, were bowed like her legs. She had a large beaky nose, a prognathous jaw jutting out like a muzzle, and no chin. Her low forehead sloped back into a long, large head, resting on a short thick neck. At the back of her head was a bony knob, an occipital bun, that emphasised its length.

A soft down of short brown hair, tending to curl, covered her legs and shoulders and ran along the upper spine of her back. It thickened into a head of heavy, long, rather bushy hair. She was already losing her winter pallor to a summer tan. Big, round, intelligent, dark brown eyes were deep set below overhanging brow ridges.

(from *The Clan of the Cave Bear* by Jean M. Auel)

"See what I mean? No sense of humour."

B What are they like?

1 Revision. Put in *always, ever, never, already* or *yet.*

1. Have you .... been to Australia?
2. I don't think she's .... got up before nine o'clock in her life.
3. Is Granny here ....?
4. 'Would you like a drink?' 'I've .... got one, thanks.'
5. I'll .... love you, darling.

6. If you are .... in New York, do come and stay.
7. .... lend money to strangers.
8. 'Is breakfast ready?' 'Not ....'
9. I .... know what I'm going to get for Christmas.
10. Do you .... have bad dreams?

2 Grammar revision: word order. Make questions for these answers. Each question should end in a preposition (e.g. *Where does your cousin come from?*).

1. I sent it to Mary. (*Who . . . ?*)
2. I was thinking about you.
3. You should eat it with a fork.
4. He bought it for his sister.

5. Why don't you put them in that big vase?
6. I'm looking for the toilets.
7. He's looking after his mother.
8. It was directed by Spielberg.

3 Vocabulary. Match the words and the faces.

cry   frown   laugh   shout   smile
stare   yawn

4 Vocabulary. Match the words and the expressions.

bored   crazy   cross   excited   happy
surprised   unhappy

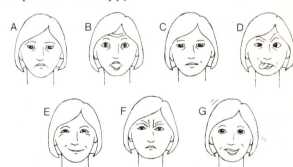

5 Write a careful description of yourself or somebody you know well. Describe both appearance and personality. Before you start writing, look back at Student's Book Lessons 22A and B.

6 Try the crossword.

19. Abbreviation for *company*.
20. Not funny.
22. Egg-shaped.
23. The opposite of *more*.
25. Do you know the difference between *such* and ....?
26. What are you looking ....?
28. Half the number of days in two weeks.
29. Would you like a cup of ....?
31. The same .... 30 down.
32. Calm and relaxed; doesn't worry about much.

DOWN
1. Loving.
2. Person who writes poetry.
3. Good at doing things.
4. As well.
5. Not asleep.
6. Red, green, blue or yellow (American spelling).
7. Why have the children got such bored .... on their faces?
13. I ...., you are, he/she is.
16. Metal.
18. It's very cold at the North ....
21. I hope you've got a good .... for taking my car without asking.
24. You sing it.
25. You sit on it.
27. Would you like another cup of ....?
30. The same .... 31 across.

ACROSS
1. The way somebody looks.
8. What are you waiting ....?
9. I don't have many .... or phobias.
10. Not awake.
11. Abbreviation for *etcetera*.
12. Kind of tree.
14. 'Who would like some more cake?' '............,'
15. Travel by bicycle or horse.
17. Journeys.

(Solution on page 138.)

"*I'm ten per cent lover, eight per cent poet and two per cent head librarian. The rest, I'm afraid, is water.*"

Keeping healthy

A They lose all of their rights

1 Vocabulary revision and extension. Match the words and the letters.

anaesthetic   anaesthetist   bandage
bedpan   chart   medical student   medicine
nurse   orderly   patient   pill   plaster
scar   screen   surgeon   syringe
thermometer   tray

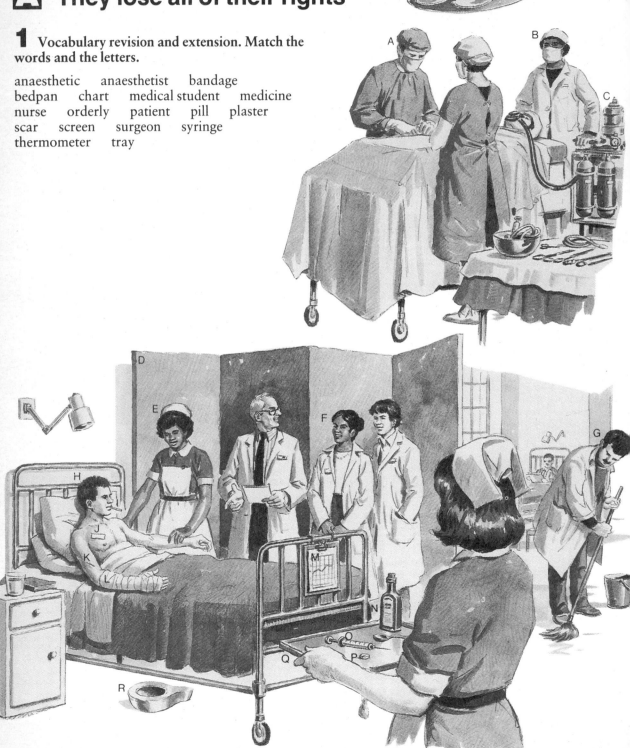

2 Grammar revision: relative pronouns. Join the pairs of sentences together as in the examples.

1. She had a heart attack. It was a great shock to her family.

   She had a heart attack, which was a great shock to her family.

2. She completely recovered from her illness. Nobody had expected this.

   She completely recovered from her illness, which nobody had expected.

3. The hospital bills were $100 a day. We couldn't afford this.
4. The nurses were all very pretty. This cheered him up a good deal.
5. He broke his leg skiing. This did not surprise us in the least.
6. He has to lie in bed all day doing nothing. He hates this.
7. Cindy sold her story to a newspaper for $10,000. This paid the hospital bills.
8. He had a terrible car crash. It put him in hospital for six months.
9. Since his accident he can't play football. He finds this terribly depressing.
10. Susy's decided to be a nurse. We're quite pleased about it.

3 Practise saying these words with the correct stress.

accident de**press**ing **hos**pital **news**paper
surgeon sur**prise** **syr**inge ther**mom**eter
uniform

4 Read the text *without* a dictionary. Then do Exercise 5.

YEE TIN MEDICAL OIL

This medical oil is a well balanced preparation, combining a number of oils of healing qualities with several curative botanical extracts.

Yee Tin Medical Oil brings immediate relief to cold, weakness in the limbs, sunstroke, phlegm, indigestion, diarrhoea and vomiting, intestinal colic, nausea, cough, heartburn, stomachache, rheumatism, gout, toothache, cramps, lumbago, cuts, sprains, swellings, boils, scabies, itches, insect bites, seasickness, trainsickness. It is also extraordinarily effective in cases of burns, cuts, insect-bites, skin irritation etc. In cases of diarrhoea and vomiting, a few drops of this oil will suffice to relieve the patient from agony. Yee Tin Medical Oil is also good for va-rious ailments among domestic animals and cattle.

Application of this oil outside the nostrils and rubbing it on the temples stimulates the nerve system. Stomachache can be relieved quickly with hard rubbing. Coughing can be eased by applying and rubbing this oil on the front part of the neck and chest. Other special merits of Yee Tin Medical Oil include stimulating circulation, quickly relieving aches and pains, soothing irritation, and easing the nasal stuffy feeling.

Be sure to have a bottle of Yee Tin Medical Oil handy, at home or on a trip. Beware of cheap imitations. Always look for the Buddha Trade Mark.

(paper accompanying medicine bought in Hong Kong)

5 Find these words and expressions in the text. Without using a dictionary, try to guess what each word means and choose the most probable explanation. When you have finished the exercise, check your answers in a dictionary.

1. curative:
   a. sweet smelling
   b. effective against illness
   c. carefully selected

2. botanical extracts:
   a. products taken from plants
   b. opinions about medicine
   c. vitamins in solid form

3. gout:
   a. a small animal
   b. a belief
   c. an illness

4. it is . . . effective:
   a. many doctors recommend it
   b. it works
   c. it is highly popular

5. irritation:
   a. anger
   b. dryness
   c. a kind of pain

6. agony:
   a. high speed
   b. a kind of snake
   c. great pain

7. ailments:
   a. kinds
   b. illnesses
   c. weakness

8. domestic:
   a. house
   b. small
   c. wild

9. temples:
   a. churches
   b. parts of the head
   c. backs of the legs

10. merits:
    a. good qualities
    b. experiences
    c. needs

6 Write a few paragraphs about one of your own experiences of hospital or illness.

"I'm afraid there's been an error, Mr Thackley – you've been cured by mistake for another patient."

"I'm afraid there's absolutely nothing I can do for you, Mr Maynard. I only handle operations over £2,500."

"Why, Mr Willis! I'm glad to see you're improving enough to sit up and fall over!"

"Provided you eat sensibly, stay off the beer, cigarettes and whisky, don't take any strenuous exercise and keep away from women you could live for another twenty minutes."

Unit 23

B Bed rest is bad for you

1 Write out one or more sections of the text, using the words in the boxes to fill the gaps.

> a great deal   germ   hospital   infection   injections   joint   pain   powerful   rub

I spent ten weeks in ....1.... once. I wouldn't want to do it again, but it was an interesting and valuable experience from which I learnt ....2.....

I had a serious ....3.... of the hip ....4...... I was rushed into hospital in great ....5...., after my doctor had finally decided that the problem was something he couldn't deal with. (He thought I had a muscle strain, and gave me some ointment to ....6.... on.) Fortunately the hospital doctors quickly identified the ....7.... that was causing the trouble, and were able to treat the infection.

After the first couple of days I felt more or less all right. I was strapped down on a frame to stop me moving the joint, and I had ....8.... penicillin ....9..... every three hours day and night, but I was reasonably comfortable.

| apparently | best | blood | bones | drugs | human beings | operations | reality | staff |
| underpaid | uniforms | ward | | | | | | |

Nobody was quite sure why it had happened, but I'd been living alone and not eating well for some time, and ....10.... lack of proper food had lowered my resistance, so that my ....11.... wasn't able to fight the infection.

I was in a ....12.... with about twenty other people. Most of them were chronic arthritis sufferers who had been in and out of hospital for years for ....13..... The surgeons did the ....14.... they could, but very few of these people could be cured. They had serious damage to their ....15.... and joints, and most of them needed ....16.... to relieve their pain.

I'll never forget the way your world shrinks in hospital. After a week or so, the only ....17.... is inside the walls of your ward. Everything outside becomes like a dream.

I developed a great admiration for the hospital ....18..... The doctors were superb, and they certainly saved my life by their prompt diagnosis and treatment. The nurses were overworked and ....19...., but they were amazingly cheerful and competent. And I found out that under those ....20.... there were some very interesting ....21.....

| damage | efforts | experience | got over | hip | illness | stiff | weak |

After eight weeks or so I was more or less cured. I was taken off the frame and allowed to start trying to walk again. At first my muscles were so ....22...., and my joints so ....23...., that I couldn't stand up, but I made enormous ....24.... to get fit again, and my strength soon came back.

I was very lucky. I came out of the hospital with nothing worse than slight ....25.... to the ....26.... joint, which has never caused me any trouble or stopped me doing what I wanted to.

I ....27.... the ....28.... relatively quickly. But the ....29.... of those ten weeks is something that I'll never get over. It wasn't a good thing to do, but in some ways it's a good thing to have done.

2 Vocabulary revision and extension. Do you know the meanings of all these words for common illnesses? Can you add any to the list?

AIDS	flu (influenza)
appendicitis	heart disease
bronchitis	malaria
cancer	measles
cholera	polio (poliomyelitis)
dysentery	tonsilitis

"I'm afraid we've done all we can do. Now it's time to play golf."

3 Grammar: passives. Make five or more sentences from the table, using *can/cannot be* + past participle. Examples:

Muscle strain can be made worse by exercise.
Muscle strain can be cured by rest.

pain	relieve	exercise
a cold	cure	aspirin
flu	mend	antibiotics
tonsilitis	make worse	an operation
appendicitis		glue
a broken bone		dieting
some illnesses		acupuncture
arthritis		drugs
weight problems		bandages
bleeding		rest
muscle strain		medicine
overtiredness		
stomachache		

4 Read the text. Then write down as quickly as you can words or expressions in the text which mean:

stays	certain	mix milk/sugar into
as well as	puts on	pull strengthened
live longer than	kill themselves	

Why men make rotten patients

Most men make dreadful patients. When they have a headache there is trouble if anyone makes a sound.

When a man has flu he lies in bed while his wife waits on him hand and foot.

When she has a pain in her chest she happily accepts being told that there is nothing seriously wrong. He remains miserable and convinced that he has heart trouble.

When he has been ordered to rest that's just what he does, complaining bitterly if there is no one around to stir his tea or find him a handkerchief. She is expected to carry on looking after the rest of the family – even though she has been told to take things easy.

In addition to being mentally less able to cope with illness men are physically not as fit as women. Men are more likely to drink, smoke and eat too much and take too little exercise.

The man who dons his tracksuit and jogs to the pub every night still does far less exercise than his wife who has to cart the groceries from the shops, handle the washing and lug the vacuum cleaner up and down stairs.

Most men know they aren't as fit as women. So when they're ill they're frightened. Their fear is reinforced by the knowledge that a woman's life expectation is longer than a man's. Although today's women drink and smoke more and take on greater responsibility than in the past, the number of years by which they can expect to outlive a man is increasing.

Men are more likely to die in accidents and of lung cancer. They're more likely to commit suicide and die of heart disease.

It's not just illness that makes men such rotten patients – it's fear!

(from an article by Dr Vernon Coleman in *The Daily Mirror*)

5 Read this. You shouldn't need a dictionary.

DOCTOR, DOCTOR
(Children's jokes)

'Doctor, please come over quickly. My wife's broken a leg.'
'But I'm a doctor of music.'
'That's OK. It's the piano leg.'

'Tell me, doctor. Is it serious?'
'Well, I wouldn't advise you to start watching any serials on TV.'

'Which do you want first – the good news or the bad news?'
'The good news, please, doctor.'
'Our tests show that you only have 24 hours to live.'
'My God – what's the bad news?'
'I should have told you last night, but I forgot.'

'Did you take those pills I gave you to improve your memory?'
'What pills?'

'Doctor, I can't stop stealing things.'
'Take these pills. They should help you.'
'But what if they don't?'
'Pick up a Rolls for me.'

'Doctor, I think I need glasses.'
'You certainly do. This is a bank.'

'Doctor I ate a dozen oysters yesterday and I've had stomachache ever since.'
'Were they fresh?'
'I don't know.'
'Well, how did they look when you opened them up?'
'You mean you're supposed to open the shells?'

'What seems to be the trouble?'
'Doctor, I keep getting the feeling that nobody can hear what I say.'
'What seems to be the trouble?'

'Doctor, I feel as if nobody ever listens to me.'
'Next, please.'

'Doctor, doctor, I keep thinking I'm a dustbin.'
'Don't talk such rubbish.'

*"Don't talk to **me** about rheumatism."*

Describing things

A Medium-sized, not small

1 Revision. Look at the examples, and then complete the sentences with *as*, *than*, *then* or *that*. Examples:

*It's about **the same** size **as** a telephone.*
*It's not quite **as** heavy **as** a TV.*
*It's a bit **bigger than** a camera.*
*I started to say something and **then** I stopped.*
*Do you think **that** she'll be all right?*

1. I'm a bit older .... I look.
2. But I'm not nearly as old .... I feel.
3. She's got the same sense of humour ....
   her mother.
4. You paid him far more .... the car was
   worth.
5. Go straight on for 300 metres and ....
   turn right.
6. Could we have the bill as soon ....
   possible, please?
7. I'm quite sure .... he's gone home.
8. Nobody's funnier .... my uncle Harry.
9. Do you think we should have the curtains
   exactly the same colour .... the carpet?
10. This year things have been better ....
    ever.

2 Modification of comparative expressions. Using expressions from both columns of the tables, compare a sheep with at least ten other things. Examples:

A sheep is not quite as intelligent as a dog.
A sheep is far slower than a jet plane.

not quite as	fast		a bit	faster
not nearly as	slow		rather	slower
nearly as	big		much	bigger
just as	small		a lot	smaller
exactly as	hard		far	harder
	soft			softer
	etc.			etc.

3 Write a description of something without saying what it is. Say as much as you can about its size and appearance. See if the teacher can work out what it is when he/she reads your description. Use words and expressions from Exercise 2 (above), and from Exercises 3 and 7 of Student's Book Lesson 24A.

4 Spelling. Write the adverbs. Examples:

quick *quickly*
nice *nicely*
easy *easily*
final *finally*
possible *possibly*

deliberate   fortunate   full   high   short
terrible   tidy   total   useful   wide

5 Read this, using a dictionary if necessary.

ELEPHANTS ARE DIFFERENT TO DIFFERENT PEOPLE
Wilson and Pilcer and Snack stood before the zoo
elephant.
   Wilson said, 'What is its name? Is it from Asia or Africa?
Who feeds it? Is it a he or a she? How old is it? Do they
have twins? How much does it cost to feed? If it dies, how
much will another one cost? If it dies, what will they use
the bones, the fat and the hide for? What use is it besides
to look at?'
   Pilcer didn't have any questions; he was murmuring to
himself, 'It's a house by itself, walls and windows, the ears
came from tall cornfields, by God; the architect of those
legs was a workman, by God; he stands like a bridge out
across deep water; the face is sad and the eyes are kind;
I know elephants are good to babies.'
   Snack looked up and down and at last said to himself,
'He's a tough son-of-a-gun outside and I'll bet he's got a
strong heart, I'll bet he's strong as a copper-riveted boiler
inside.'
   They didn't put up any arguments.
   They didn't throw anything in each other's faces.
   Three men saw the elephant three ways
   And let it go at that.
   They didn't spoil a sunny Sunday afternoon;
   'Sunday comes only once a week,' they told each
other.

(from *Home Front Memo* by Carl Sandburg)

6 **Which caption do you think goes with which cartoon?**

"You won't remember me, but I called in to see
   you next week and you were busy . . ."

"It's the office. Shall I tell them you're sick?"

"You have a go in ours, and we'll have a go in
   yours. OK?"

"Personally, I think it's rather cruel, keeping them
   in those little round bowls."

"There are two sides to every argument, George,
   and I've already presented them both."

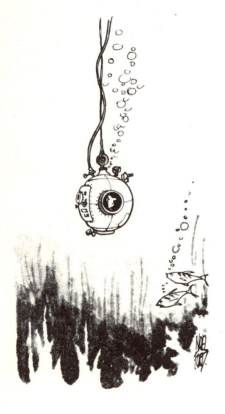

B Guaranteed used cars

1 Vocabulary revision and extension. Do you know the names of the main parts of a car? Match the words and the numbers.

accelerator (pedal)   bonnet (*American* hood)
boot (*American* trunk)   brake pedal
bumper   clutch pedal   dashboard   engine
gear lever (*American* gear shift)
handbrake (*American* emergency brake)
headlight   indicator light   mirror
petrol tank (*American* gas tank)   radiator
roof rack   seat   seat belt
speedometer   steering wheel
windscreen (*American* windshield)   wiper

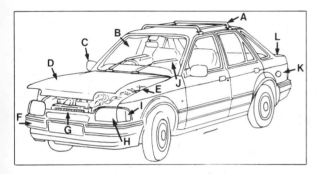

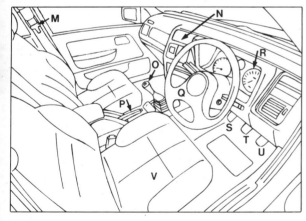

2 Look again at Exercise 3 in Student's Book Lesson 24B. Then use some of the structures to compare one or more of the following pairs of things.

two cars, motorbikes, bicycles or aeroplanes
two different means of transport (e.g. bus and train)
two different buildings that you know
two makes of record player, cassette player, TV or computer

3 Read the letter, and rewrite it putting in commas, full stops, question marks, apostrophes and capital letters where necessary.

```
                              14 hillside road
                              dover
                              12 december 1987

dear sir

i am writing to complain about the car that i
bought from you yesterday it is just a heap of
scrap when i tried to start it this morning the
key wouldnt turn in the lock the battery was
flat and two of the plugs needed changing then
when i finally got it going the bonnet wouldnt
stay closed and the drivers side door fell off
and when i tried to stop to pick up the door the
brakes didnt work so i crashed into a tree and
smashed the radiator also one of the wheels came
off

do you really think this car is worth £150 well
if you do i dont what are you going to do about
it

yours faithfully

eric smith
```

4 EITHER: Write an advertisement for something you want to sell.
    OR: Write a letter of complaint (better expressed than the one above) about something you have bought that doesn't work.

5 Read this with a dictionary (it is taken from a book published 50 years ago).

EXAMINATION
Parking Limit – Two Hours.
Write on one side of the road only.

(a) *Mechanics*
Your car, except for a tendency to slow down on hills, runs perfectly all day.
   On starting it up next morning, however, you find that it will only move a few inches. What would you do?
Answer: Open the garage door.

(b) *History*
Describe the difference between roads made by the Romans and those constructed nowadays.
Answer: The roads made by the Romans have lasted until the present time.

(c) *English grammar*
What is wrong with the following: 'When I got to the crossroads I hooted and slowed down and looked to see if it was safe to cross'?
Answer: It isn't true.

(d) *General knowledge*
1. Why is a red light used for danger?
Answer: Because a bright colour that cannot be confused with anything else is essential.
2. Why is a red light used for advertising restaurants, cinemas, drink, shops, pills and everything else?
Answer: See above.

(e) *Legal*
A motorist comes suddenly out of a small side road, dashes straight across a main line of traffic against the lights, mounts the pavement, runs right up the steps of a public house, crashes through the door and finally comes to rest hard up against the bar. Is he breaking the law?
Answer: No, not unless he has his car with him.

(from *You have been warned* by Fougasse and McCullough)

FASTER THAN A FERRARI.
Travelling flat out at 71.5mph the Citroën 2CV will easily overtake the Ferrari Mondial travelling at 65mph.

AS MANY WHEELS AS A ROLLS ROYCE.
The £55,240 Rolls-Royce Silver Spirit. How many wheels? Four. The £2,584 Citroën 2CV. How many wheels? Exactly the same.

MORE ROOM THAN A PORSCHE.
With a possible 30cu. ft. boot space there's no need for one of those plastic luggage racks on our little run-about.

THE £2,584 CITROËN 2CV.
All you'll ever need in a car.

(advertisement for Citroën cars)
(*Note:* Prices correct in 1984.)

"I'm having some trouble with the car I just rented from you – the wipers don't work properly."

Telling the truth

A Freedom of information

1 Vocabulary. Complete the text with words and expressions from the box.

correct	democratic	employment
individual	obtain	opinions	private
protect	public	right	

The citizen's need to know is not confined to .....1..... affairs. It arises also in his .....2..... and family life, his .....3....., the education of his children, the health and social security of his family, and justice to them all. In short, a free .....4..... society requires that the law should recognise and .....5..... the .....6..... of the .....7..... to the information necessary to make his own choices and decisions on public and private matters, to express his own .....8....., and to be able himself to act to .....9..... injustice to himself or his family. None of these rights can be fully effective unless he can .....10..... information.

(Lord Scarman)

2 Revision: countable and uncountable nouns.

Countable nouns have plurals, and can be used with the article *a/an*. Examples:
law (a law, laws)
choice (a choice, choices)
Uncountable nouns have no plurals, and usually cannot be used with the article *a/an*. Examples:
health
information (you cannot say *an information* or *informations* in English)

Can you divide these nouns into countable and uncountable, and write them in two lists? Use a good dictionary to check your answers.

affair   choice   decision   education
exception   health   information   justice
law   right   security   society

Examples:

COUNTABLE	UNCOUNTABLE
law	health
choice	information
....	....

3 Pronunciation. Practise saying these words with the correct stress (they are all stressed on the second syllable).

allow   apply   autho**ri**ty   committee
correct   de**part**ment   exception   majority
ob**tain**   official   pro**tect**

4 Read one or more of these three texts.

I found out a year ago (by accident) that the notes at a hospital I attended had words to this effect: 'this woman has a history of mental illness'. I was too shocked to say anything to the doctor; she doesn't even know that I saw it.
  I have *never* had, or asked for, a sleeping pill or any drug for nerves etc.
  I now feel that doctors tend to ignore what I say to them until it's too late. I can't help feeling that whoever wrote this on my notes has *not* helped me in any way. I am not a nervous person in any way. Nor do I go to the doctor with minor complaints.
  Is there any way I can find out why this was written in my notes?

(from a letter to the Campaign for Freedom of Information)

A twenty-year-old student visited a doctor at a university medical centre asking for treatment for a facial rash. After consulting his medical notes, the doctor asked him if he needed another prescription for his tablets. The student asked what tablets these were. The doctor replied that, according to the records, he was taking anti-convulsants. The student denied it. The doctor checked his notes again. They stated that the student had been operated on for the removal of a brain tumour; that 'since then he has been subject to grand mal convulsions'; and that he required daily medication to control the problem. The student denied that any of this was true.
  The university doctor then contacted the student's previous doctor, and later received the following reply: 'On checking through our records I have discovered that the details regarding temporal lobotomy (the brain operation) relate to another patient of ours. Perhaps you would be kind enough to delete the wrong information and accept my apologies.'

(from a report by the Campaign for Freedom of Information)

▶

115

A girl who changed schools was described, in the report sent to the new school, as 'a thief and a liar and sly'. Her teacher at the new school said that she seemed honest, truthful, frank and extremely helpful. Other comments on children's files by teachers have included the following:

– 'Parents are not married.' (they were)
– 'A high IQ (intelligence quotient) figure, surprising in a child from a dull family.'
– 'This boy is big, black and smelly.'
– 'I believe he is moving inexorably towards a life of crime and terms of imprisonment. He affects a nice side to his character but this is not genuine.'

(from a report by the Campaign for Freedom of Information)

5 Write a few paragraphs about one or more of the following questions.

1. Do you feel that people should always be allowed to see their medical records?
2. Should schoolchildren and/or their parents be allowed to see the children's educational files?
3. Should people have a right to see all the information that is in their files at the bank?
4. What about police and military files?

"You are accused of something. As it affects national security, I am not at liberty to say what it is. How do you plead?"

Unit 25

B Would you ever lie?

1 Grammar: 'unreal' past tenses. Put in suitable verbs from the box.

| could   knew   meant (twice)   thought   wanted (twice)   were (twice) |

Suppose you could read people's minds, so that you always .....1..... what they .....2..... thinking. You would know when people .....3..... lying to you, or if they .....4..... to cheat you, for example. And you would be able to see what politicians really .....5..... when they were making all their promises. It would be useful in exams, too, because you .....6..... find out the answers by reading the examiners' minds. And when people said 'I love you', you could find out if they really .....7..... it. But in general I think I would prefer not to know things that people .....8..... to keep secret. And I'm not sure that I would really want to know everything that people .....9..... about me.

2 Vocabulary revision. Look at the picture and match the words in the list with the numbers.

ridge   field   gate   glacier   hill   island   lake   mountain   path   river   road
rocks   stream   valley   waterfall   wood

3 Read one or more of the following texts.

The first casualty when war comes is truth.

(Hiram Johnson)

For secrets are edged tools
And must be kept from children and from fools.

(Dryden)

The problems of policing Calne were discussed at a secret meeting last night between local councillors, Mayor Mr Ted Cooper and Chief Superintendent Sam Ashley, divisional head of Chippenham police. But no one would release any information today. Mr Cooper said, 'It was conducted in private because it concerned the public so much.'

(report in *The Bristol Evening Post*)

In England it is bad manners to be clever, to assert something confidently. It may be your personal view that two and two make four, but you must not state it in a self-assured way, because this is a democratic country and others may be of a different opinion.
. . . People on the Continent either tell you the truth or lie; in England they hardly ever lie, but they would not dream of telling you the truth.

(George Mikes)

Well, I think lying is a very basic sin, however you look at it and however you laugh about it. I just think lying is bad, and I would rather not say anything. I can't lie without it being obvious. I think lying is on a par with thieving. You know, I feel quite strongly about it. I don't believe in sort of white lies. I think it's better not to say anything. In fact, I avoid saying things if I feel I've got to lie. So I don't lie.

(Marilyn Norvell)

Have you ever noticed, friend, that when you are sleeping happily and the telephone rings and you reach an arm from under the blanket and say 'Hello' into the mouthpiece, the voice on the telephone always says 'Did I wake you up?'
And have you ever noticed how you immediately and invariably reply? You lie. 'Of course not,' you say, or 'Are you kidding? I've been up for hours.'
Scientific studies with laboratory mice have not yet shown how many persons will answer candidly – 'Yes, you woke me up, and I hope you're satisfied' – but I bet it is fewer than three in a million.

(Russell Baker)

4 Can you solve this problem?

One of the children broke a window. When they were questioned, they answered as follows. They were all lying. Who broke the window?

ANDREW: It was Dan.
BILL: It wasn't me, it was either Carol or Eric.
CAROL: It was me.
DAN: It was either Andrew or Carol.
ERIC: It was either Andrew or Dan.

"You have an honest face, sir – open 'em up!"

"Don't lie to me – you've been to the pub again."

5 How honest are you? Read the questionnaire and answer the questions.

1. Have you ever avoided paying the fare while travelling on a bus or train?
   a. Often.
   b. Occasionally.
   c. Never.

2. If you saw a purse or wallet lying in the road, would you:
   a. pick it up and take it home?
   b. take it to the police station?
   c. ask people around if it is theirs, and if not, keep it?

3. Have you ever taken anything from a shop without paying for it?
   a. Once.
   b. More than once.
   c. Never.

4. If you broke a vase in someone's home, would you:
   a. tell the owner immediately?
   b. blame the cat?
   c. say you knew nothing about it?

5. Suppose you sometimes earned money which it was possible to hide from the taxman. Would you:
   a. always avoid paying tax?
   b. declare some, but not all, of the money?
   c. never avoid paying tax?

6. Have you ever pretended to be ill to get off work or school?
   a. Once.
   b. Frequently.
   c. Never.

7. If you were buying two items in a shop and were only charged for one, would you point it out and pay the correct amount?
   a. Yes.
   b. No.

8. If you were brought the wrong bill in a restaurant, and the bill you were given was less than yours, would you:
   a. point it out to the waiter?
   b. quickly pay and get out?
   c. pay it and casually stroll out, saying, if asked, that you hadn't noticed?

9. Have you ever given the impression that you had more money than you actually have?
   a. Yes, often.
   b. Occasionally.
   c. Never.

10. If you bought a coat and accidentally made a mark on it, would you:
    a. keep the coat and try and remove the mark?
    b. take the coat back to the shop and complain that there was a mark on it?
    c. take the coat back saying it was the wrong size, and ask for your money back or an exchange without mentioning the mark?

(See score table and comments after Exercise 6.)

6 Write a few paragraphs about one or both of the following questions.

1. Do you think it is always wrong to lie? Why (not)?
2. If you only had a short time to live, would you want to know? Why (not)?

HOW HONEST ARE YOU?

Give yourself 1 point for each correct answer.

1. c 2. b 3. c 4. a 5. c 6. c 7. a 8. a
9. c 10. a

TOTAL 8–10: You are a very honest person and completely trustworthy. You dislike dishonesty in others and hate being deceived.

TOTAL 3–7: You are fairly honest, but you have a dishonest streak in you. You do not consciously set out to deceive people, but if the situation arises you may take the opportunity to gain something from acting dishonestly.

TOTAL 0–2: Cheating is a game for you. If you can get something without paying for it, you will do so. If somebody else suffers, you think that it is their fault for being less smart than you. You are a pretty dishonest person.

Sport

A They are incredible runners

1 Make sure you know what the words in the box mean. If necessary, look at the advertisement on page 107 of the Student's Book again to see how they are used. Then fill in the gaps in the text. You may have to make some small changes. There is one word too many.

altogether	approximately	average	breathe
chilly	comfortable	confident	continuously
distance	extraordinary	incredible	last (verb)
opportunity	period	prove	race	reason
valley	wear	win	

I was on holiday in the mountains, and I saw a notice advertising a cycle ....1..... I used to do a lot of cycling, but I had never been in a race before, so I thought I would have a try. It was an .....2.... to show what I could do – to .....3.... to myself that I could still ride a bike.

On the morning of the race the weather was .....4...... So I decided to .....5.... warm clothing – it might slow me down a bit, but I felt more .....6.... of finishing if I was .....7..... I was very nervous, especially when I saw the other competitors. There were about eighty riders .....8....., and most of them looked as if they did this sort of thing twice a week.

The course was very hilly. We started in a deep .....9....., climbed out over a mountain pass, and then went up and down .....10..... for a .....11.... of .....12.... 50 miles. I felt quite good at the beginning, but it didn't .....13..... After the first five miles my leg muscles were on fire, I found it difficult to .....14...., and most of the other riders were out of sight. The speed was .....15....: on some of the downhill stretches I must have .....16.... 60 miles per hour.

Something .....17.... happened towards the end. For some .....18...., although I was very tired, I started feeling really good. My breathing got much easier, and on one steep downhill section I started to sing.

I didn't .....19....., of course, but I wasn't last. I was last but one, actually. The rider who came in behind me – three seconds behind me, to be precise – was twelve years old. It was her first race as well, so we shook hands and congratulated each other on finishing.

The next day I couldn't walk.

2 Grammar: prepositions in relative clauses. Look at the examples of formal and informal relative structures, and then change the expressions to make them more or less formal. Examples:

the clothes (that) you're running in (informal)
the clothes in which you are running (formal)

the people (that) he went with (informal)
the people with whom he went (formal)

1. **Make these expressions informal:**
   the woman at whom you are looking
   the people to whom you were talking
   the problem about which she was worried
   the person for whom he bought it
   the game in which he played

2. **Make these expressions formal:**
   the house she lives in
   the people you're talking about
   the man she was living with
   the people I work with
   the building I work in

3 Grammar: structures with *keep*.

Clothes **keep you warm**. Good shoes **keep your feet comfortable**. TV **keeps the children quiet**. What do the following do?

– gloves
– an umbrella
– a fridge
– central heating
– air conditioning
– a toothbrush
– vitamins
– regular exercise
– black coffee
– toys

4 Revision: two- and three-word verbs. Use the expressions in the box to complete the sentences. You may have to make some small changes. There is one extra expression – can you make a sentence with it?

get on	get on with	get up	go on
look after	look at	look out	put off
put on	ring back	run out of	
slow down	turn on		

1. If you .... talking like that I'm leaving.
2. She's really nice – she .... everybody.
3. You're going too fast – could you .... a bit?
4. I'll have to .... going to the dentist – I haven't got time this week.
5. Could you .... the radio so that we can hear the news?
6. ....! You're going to knock that glass off the table.
7. I don't much like .... children.
8. After we had been travelling for about half an hour, I began to realise that I .... the wrong train.
9. I'm a bit busy just now. Can I .... in ten minutes?
10. It's cold outside. I think I'll .... a sweater.
11. .... those clouds. I think it's going to rain.
12. I've .... sugar. Could you lend me some?

5 Read this with a dictionary.

BELIEVE IT OR NOT
Sky-divers fall at speeds of up to 300km per hour.
In pelota (a game played in the Basque provinces of Spain) the ball can travel at 290km per hour.
The American wrestler William J. Cobb weighed 363kg in 1962.
The South African swimmer Karen Muir broke a world record when she was 12.
Joy Foster was Jamaican table tennis champion in 1958, at the age of 8.
Oscar G. Swahn, from Sweden, won a silver medal for shooting in the 1920 Olympic Games at the age of 72.
The American boxer Muhammad Ali won $6½ million for a single fight in 1976.
Over 50,000 runners may take part in the 'Stramilano', a 22km race round Milan.
Britain's most popular active sport is fishing.
In 1974 Lynn Nolan Ryan threw a baseball at 162km per hour.
The cyclist Tommy Godwin rode 120,805km in the year 1939 – an average of 330km per day.

6 Do you like playing or watching any sport or game? Write a few lines about it.

"I gather the Queen's taken up jogging."

B 'Man of the Match'

1 Grammar: reported speech. Look at the extract from the interview with Trevor Hebberd, and the following report. Then write your own report of the next part of the interview.

INTERVIEW
It's not what people think it is. I mean, you would, all you do is, you do all the dirty jobs, you have to clean people's boots, you have to pick up their kit, wash out the bathrooms, scrub the floors, it's – things like that. Paint walls. We were doing all that sort of thing.

> REPORT
> He said that life for a young professional footballer wasn't what people thought it was. All they did was the dirty jobs: they had to clean people's boots, pick up their kit, wash out the bathrooms, scrub the floors, paint walls and things like that.

INTERVIEW
Some of the travelling isn't too – too good. I mean, going up on a Friday night and staying in a hotel. It's all right, but it's not – you know, I mean, it takes you away from your family and your kids a little bit. Sometimes training can be very monotonous. I mean, that's a thing you have to put up with, but I think certain things you have to do in training are very boring.

> REPORT
> ....

2 Write a report of a conversation that you have had recently.

3 Vocabulary revision and extension. Can you put the words in groups? Some words will go in more than one group. Can you add any words?

backstroke   board   breast stroke   bridge
chess   club   court   crawl   diamonds
football   goal   goalkeeper   golf   hearts
hole   ice hockey   net   pass   queen
racket   referee   rink   serve   skate
skiing   slalom   slope   stick   swimming
tennis   trump   umpire

4 Look at the questions and then see how quickly you can find the answers in the text.

1. Which team won the match?
2. What colour were they wearing?
3. What team were Harris and Carrick playing for?
4. Were Carrick and Saunders on the same side?
5. Who scored Merton's goal?
6. Did Carrick score?

MERTON CITY V NEW PARK RANGERS
(*Extracts from a TV commentary*)

. . . and so it's Merton City in the dark blue stripes who kick off . . . that's Harris . . . that's Carrick . . . Keith Dawson wearing number 6 . . . Littlecote in there challenging . . .

. . . throw again for New Park . . .

. . . goal kick . . . that's Barrow . . . good ball, a good chance – it's a goal! A beautiful ball through by Peter Carrick and then Saunders number 10, makes it one goal to nil for Merton.

. . . and Dawson trying to find . . . and almost got through . . . Steve Rukin with the interception . . . away by Delaney . . .

. . . now it's Keith Dawson – and Rangers are really keeping up the pressure in these last ten minutes of the first half . . . neat, very neat – Carrick got the return ball . . . and Carrick still going . . . and Carrick with a shot! . . .

Tring with a cross . . . Hutchins coming in . . . away by Delaney . . . that's Rukin, to Barrow . . . corner . . .

. . . and that's the whistle for half-time with Merton City leading by one goal to nil.

. . . Tring . . . free kick – two Park players and another . . . and it almost went in – it must have hit the post and rebounded – what a remarkable piece of luck for City!

. . . one minute to go of playing time . . . throw in to Merton City . . . it's a corner – could this be the last corner of the match? . . . the whistle has blown – and Merton City has knocked New Park Rangers out of the FA Cup – a great great victory by Merton City.

5 Try the crossword.

ACROSS
1. I'd like to have an .... to go to Australia.
6. I can't go this year, because I've .... time or money.
8. In 1939, Tommy Godwin cycled an .... of 330km a day for a year.
12. Not well.
13. Trevor Hebberd is a .... footballer.
16. Past of the verb *speed*.
17. Trevor Hebberd is a professional ....
18. We use *a* before a consonant and .... before a vowel.
19. Chess isn't as physically tiring .... football.

21. Person who cleans.
23. Why don't you .... and jump in the river?
24. If you .... the number of days in a week and the number of weeks in a month, you get the number of people in a football team.
25. The opposite of *off*, backwards.
27. The goalkeeper is the person who plays .... goal.
28. Unbelievable.

DOWN
1. The opposite of *yes*, backwards.
2. I like classical music but I don't like .... music.
3. When a professional footballer reaches 30 he's already getting too ....
4. Read something in one language and write it in another.
5. Person who trains a sportsman.
7. Contraction of *he will*.
9. Happy.
10. What time do you get .... in the morning?
11. Engine.
14. Land surrounded by water.
15. The opposite of *closed*.
17. You may have a ring on this.
20. The past of *shine*.
21. Part of your face below your mouth.
22. Abbreviation for *Automobile Association*.
25. Zero score in football.
26. I can't go to Australia because I haven't got any time .... money.

(*Solution on page 138.*)

"*Remember, son – let the ball do the work.*"

Plans

A   I'm afraid this is going to come as a shock

1 Spelling revision. Write the *-ing* forms. What are the rules?

start – starting	take
hope – hoping	wait
stop – stopping	send
get	run
jump	come
like	sit
rub	

Three weeks today . . .

2 Grammar: future progressive tense. Look at the pictures and write sentences to say what the person will be doing at the different times. Example:

This time tomorrow he will be flying to the USA.

This time tomorrow . . .

In two weeks . . .

This time next week . . .

Two days from now . . .

Three days from now . . .

In five days . . .

3 Say what you will (or might) be doing at some of these times:

in two hours' time	in six months
eight hours from now	this time next year
this time tomorrow	two years from now
this time next Tuesday	five years from now
three weeks tomorrow	

4 Grammar: future perfect tense. Look at the work schedule and say what the situation will be at the following times: mid-March, the end of April, mid-June, early September. Example:

By mid-February they will just have started the runways, they will have built most of the approach road, they will have finished the foundations for Terminal 1, but they won't have started Terminal 2.

EAST MERTON AIRPORT WORK SCHEDULE

OCT	NOV	DEC	JAN	FEB	MAR	APR	MAY	JUN	JUL	AUG	SEPT	OCT	NOV	DEC	JAN

work on approach road

work on runways

foundations for Terminal 1

construction of Terminal 1 building

foundations for Terminal 2

construction of Terminal 2 building

control tower

5 Write sentences about things which you will have started or finished by some of the following times (or other times if you prefer):

three hours from now	two years from now
three months from now	five years from now
by next year	ten years from now

6 Read your horoscope with a dictionary.

YOUR STARS

AQUARIUS (Jan. 21–Feb. 18)
This time tomorrow you'll be doing something you've never done in your life before. Try to get it right. Money could be a problem towards the end of the week. Look out for trouble from small animals.

PISCES (Feb. 19–Mar. 20)
Stop being so sorry for yourself. Everybody's getting fed up with you. Even the cat is getting fed up with you. If you go on like this, you'll have lost all your friends by the end of the year.

ARIES (Mar. 21–Apr. 20)
Wonderful things are going to happen to you this week. One of your poems will be published in a gardening magazine. A friend will send you a postcard. Friday will bring an invitation to a folk concert. Enjoy the excitement while it lasts; next week everything will be back to normal.

TAURUS (Apr. 21–May 21)
Years ago, you treated somebody very badly. You thought they'd forgotten? No. They'll be looking for revenge this week. Don't try to get away: there is no place to hide.

GEMINI (May 22–June 21)
Prepare for travel. Some very strange things are going to happen, and you are suddenly going to become President of a small distant oil-rich country. This time next week you'll be sitting in the Palace drinking champagne.

CANCER (June 22–July 22)
This week's problem will be children. By the end of the week you'll be wishing they had all been drowned at birth. Try to be patient; next week will bring more children.

LEO (July 23–Aug. 23)
A tall handsome man wearing a uniform will come into your life. This may mean a visit to the police station. Tell the truth – it's better in the end.

VIRGO (Aug. 24–Sept. 23)
First, the good news. Somebody you have always been strongly attracted to will be sending you an invitation. Now the bad news: it's to a wedding. Not yours.

LIBRA (Sept. 24–Oct.23)
At last your talent, beauty, intelligence and human warmth are going to be properly recognised. By Friday you'll be rich and famous; by Saturday you'll already have been on TV three times; this time next week you'll be starting a glamorous new career.

SCORPIO (Oct. 24–Nov. 22)
Tomorrow will bring an enormous sum of money out of the blue. It's a pity you're so extravagant – by this time next week you'll probably have spent it all.

SAGITTARIUS (Nov. 23–Dec. 21)
Be careful in your relationships. In the great supermarket of life, you have to pay for anything you break – including hearts. Try to say 'No' more often. You are too attractive for your own good.

CAPRICORN (Dec. 22–Jan. 20)
Thursday is a bad day for travel. Friday is a bad day for meetings. Saturday is a bad day for everything. You'll have got over the worst by Sunday, but stay cautious – fate could still have a few unpleasant surprises for you.

7 Write a horoscope for somebody you don't like, and one for somebody you like.

B I'm a bit short of time these days

1 Vocabulary revision. Can you write the names of all the months in English?

2 Vocabulary revision. Can you write the times?

 A B C

ten past three   twenty to four

 D E F

 G H I

3 If today is Tuesday August 9, what day and date are the following?

the day after tomorrow	three weeks tomorrow
a week today	a week ago yesterday
tomorrow week	a week ago tomorrow
Thursday week	two weeks from now

If today is Monday August 15, then Wednesday August 17 is *the day after tomorrow.* **What expressions could you use to talk about the following days?**

Saturday August 13	Monday August 8
Tuesday August 23	Sunday August 7
Thursday August 25	Tuesday August 9
Tuesday August 30	

4 Pronunciation. Copy the words and underline the stressed syllables.

apprentice   average   continuously
disagreeable   extraordinary   incredible
opportunity   performance   pressure
reorganisation   talented   translator
unbelievable   unless

5 Write the other side of this telephone conversation. You can change some of the answers if you want to.

Hello, Carlingford 71661.

....

Speaking.

....

I'm not sure. Let me just look in my diary. Yes, I think so.

....

Well, I don't know.

....

Are you sure?

....

Why?

....

I don't think I'd like that.

....

No. Anyway, I really ought to wash my hair.

....

No, I'm going to the theatre.

....

I'm not sure.

....

She's not in.

....

I don't know.

....

No.

....

Goodbye.

6 Write about your plans for the next five years.

7 **Read the poems with a dictionary.**

DAYS

What are days for?
Days are where we live.
They come, they wake us
Time and time over.
They are to be happy in:
Where can we live but days?

Ah, solving that question
Brings the priest and the doctor
In their long coats
Running over the fields.

(Philip Larkin)

"Are we doing anything on Tuesday week?"

DAYS

MONDAY
You'd better not try anything
just don't try anything
that's all.
You're all the same
you days.
Give you an inch . . .
Well
I've got my eye on you
and I'm feeling light
fast
and full of aggro
so just watch it
OK?

TUESDAY
Listen, Tuesday
I'm sorry
I wasn't very nice to you.
It was *sweet* of you
to give me all those stars
when you said goodbye.
They must have cost a fortune
and they really were
just
what I've always wanted.

WEDNESDAY
Cracks, spills, burns, bills, broken cups,
    stains, wrong numbers, missed trains:
you're doing it on purpose
aren't you?
Trying it on
to see how far you can go.
I swear to you
if the phone rings again
while I'm in the bath
I'll pull it out
and ram it down your throat.

THURSDAY
'A difficult day for Aries
caution is advisable
in business dealings
setbacks possible
in affairs of the heart.'
Thursday, my friend
if we've got to get
through all these hours together
we might as well do it
with as little trouble as possible.
You keep to your side of the horoscope
and I'll keep to mine.

FRIDAY
Day like a shroud
ten feet down
black
in an airless coffin
you wrap me
in my own
clinging
loathsome
sticky skin.
I scream
and you laugh.

SATURDAY
Day
oh day
I love your perfume
(you put on daffodils
just for me)
and your yellow eye
sparkling
and the sexy way
you rub up
against me
day
I love you.

SUNDAY
Sunday and I
got drunk together
and you know
it turns out
we went to the same school.
He's a bit strange at first
but actually
he's not a bad chap
when you get to know him
old Sunday.

(Lewis Mancha)

Family and roots

A Exiles

1 Use the words and expressions in the box to complete the text.

abroad	advantages	area	as well
at home	community	contact	generation
local	miss	passed on	relations
roots	various	way of life

I can't say I really feel ....1.... anywhere. I was born in a city, but I hate cities. I love mountains, but I've never lived in mountain country: my home is in a flat agricultural ....2.... in the south of England which I find boring. I don't have much in common with the ....3.... people, and my ....4.... is very different from theirs, so I don't feel that I'm really part of the ....5.....

Although I'm English, in some ways I don't feel English. I've spent time in ....6.... countries, and I can happily live ....7.... for a period. Not for ever, though. In the end I always begin to feel too foreign, and ....8.... too many things. It's then that I realise that my ....9.... really are in England, even if I can't say exactly where.

I don't have very strong family ties, and I'm not in ....10.... with many of my relatives. My Canadian wife has a much stronger sense of family, which she has ....11.... to our son. His home and his immediate family mean a great deal to him, and his extended family is very important to him ....12..... He's very fond of all his Canadian ....13...., and likes to see them as often as he can.

So perhaps the next ....14.... will have more roots than I have. In some ways I hope so, but being rootless has ....15.... too. On balance, I'm not sure that I'd prefer to belong to one place, one community and one set of ideas.

2 Grammar revision: conditionals. Complete the text with past or conditional forms of the verbs in the box. You can use verbs more than once, and you may need to use negative forms.

| be | give up | go on | feel | have | miss |
| succeed | try | understand | use |

How _would_ _you_ _feel_ if you _had_ to live abroad for the rest of your life? Do you think you ....1.... unhappy? Are there any things that you ....2.... in particular? Suppose you ....3.... children who grew up speaking a foreign language instead of your own. How ....4.... you ....5....? Do you think that you would feel that you ....6.... them? ....7.... you ....8.... to preserve something of your culture and way of life? And ....9.... you ....10.... to pass this on to your children? Do you think you ....11....? ....12.... you ....13.... speaking your own language, or ....14.... you ....15.... using it? Would you be afraid of forgetting it if you ....16.... it?

3 Match verbs from the first list with objects from the second. Example:

take off clothes

break off   bring up   cut up   give up
look up   ring up   take off   turn off
turn over   work out   write down

address   children   clothes   friend   light
meat   page   problem   relationship
smoking   words

4 Read the text with a dictionary.

What is it to love someone if you don't share the same mother-tongue? My companion's English is reasonably good; infinitely better than my Russian. But many of the fine shades of meaning that would normally be possible in a conversation between two intimately connected people are out of reach. Do our nerve endings converse more intelligently by way of compensation; do we know by instinct most of the things that must be unsaid or imperfectly understood? In a sentimental mood, I'd say yes. But at the back of my mind is always the notion that you can only understand someone when you understand how, on the deepest level, they make use of language.

Sometimes I gaze at the optimistic row of Russian primers, readers and dictionaries on my bookshelf and think: but it will never be the language of my infancy, my school-days, my first loves, it will never truly be mine – just as English will never be truly his. And so there will always be something about each other we don't know. My mother and he agree on one thing – that my poems are incomprehensible. So the best of me is closed to him. But the best isn't good enough. If he could read me so well he'd know all my faults, human as well as literary. It would pin me down. I write more freely, knowing that I can never either fulfil or disappoint the expectations of those who truly love me.

Sometimes I feel as if I have no language at all, that my country is called Nowhere. For example – we're listening to Radio Svoboda, and I must either interrupt every few seconds to ask the meaning of this and that, or understand practically nothing. I sit silently, knowing that

it's a programme about dissident writers which I would lap up greedily if only I could . . . I concentrate on my food or my thoughts or read an English newspaper in which the words are somehow like dead insects. I am a foreigner. I am a little island of Englishness in this Russian kitchen. It is the same when he entertains friends or talks to them on the phone – I think: they make him laugh in a way I never can, and a cold, ugly jealousy comes down on me like fog. And yet my own culture is all around me in the world outside, and his is not: how dare I begrudge him a few moments when a warm voice holds exile at bay? Perhaps it's because I don't feel I belong in the world outside either. This Russian kitchen in an English flat, this nowhere language made of English-Russian and Russian-English and silence, these stories we tell one another about our unimaginable pasts – these are home.

Just before the O-level exam which I took recently, I began to dream in Russian. I don't know how ungrammatical or even nonsensical it was, but in the dream at least, it looked or sounded OK. One night I found myself reading through an O-level translation text. It was about an old man who lived in a big house that had once been a hotel: he grew strawberries in the garden, as I distinctly remember. Public-spiritedly, I divulged my dream in advance to my fellow candidates, but, to our chagrin, the passage the universities' board came up with was about a young doctor called Vera who hated flying. At any rate, I consoled myself, something of the language must have filtered through to my subconscious mind if I can dream in it . . . there is hope for me yet . . .

(from *Dreaming in a Foreign Language* by Carol Rumens)

5 Write a few lines in answer to one or more of the following questions.

1. Have you ever experienced anything like the situation of the writer of the text in Exercise 4?
2. Why do you think that the writer's companion, who is a Russian living in England, surrounds himself with Russian things? Would you behave like this if you lived abroad?
3. What would you miss most if you had to live abroad for the rest of your life?
4. If you were married to a foreigner and had to live abroad, would you try to bring up your children in the culture and traditions of your own country?

Unit 28

B I knew everyone

1 Vocabulary revision. How quickly can you answer these questions?

Your father's or mother's brother is called your *uncle*. What is the word for each of these?

- your father's or mother's sister
- your uncle's wife
- your brother's or sister's son
- your brother's or sister's daughter
- your sister's husband

- your brother's wife
- your son's wife
- your wife's or husband's father
- your uncle's son or daughter

2 Grammar revision: possessives. How quickly can you write the answers?

Your nephew is *your brother's or sister's son*. How could you describe each of these?

– your aunt
– your uncle
– your niece
– your cousin
– your grandson
– your mother-in-law
– your sister-in-law

3 Grammar revision. Put in *for, since, from* or *ago*.

1. I've known her .... seven years.
2. But I've only known her well .... last year.
3. She joined my firm about ten years ....
4. But she was away at the New York branch .... 1984 to 1986.
5. .... January she's been in charge of the marketing division.
6. I had known .... some time that she was going to get the job.
7. In fact, she should have had it years ...., but they couldn't get old Harrison out.
8. It was pretty obvious .... her first few weeks in the new job that she was going to be first class.
9. In fact, she should turn out to be the best marketing manager the firm's had .... a very long time – maybe .... the 1950s.

4 Grammar: position of prepositions.

A chair is **something to sit on**.
A hammer is **something to hit nails with**.

Write definitions of: a fork, a knife, a pen, writing paper, a platform, glasses, a toy, a cup, a bed.

5 Read this without a dictionary if possible. (*Alien* means 'foreigner'.)

ONCE A FOREIGNER, ALWAYS A FOREIGNER
I believe, without undue modesty, that I have certain qualifications to write on 'how to be an alien'. I am an alien myself. What is more, I have been an alien all my life. Only during the first twenty-six years of my life I was not aware of this plain fact. I was living in my own country, a country full of aliens, and I noticed nothing peculiar or irregular about myself; then I came to England, and you can imagine my painful surprise.

Like all great and important discoveries it was a matter of a few seconds. You probably all know from your schooldays how Isaac Newton discovered the law of gravitation. An apple fell on his head. This incident set him thinking for a minute or two, then he exclaimed joyfully: 'Of course! The gravitation constant is the acceleration per second that a mass of one gram causes at a distance of one centimetre.' You were also taught that James Watt one day went into the kitchen where cabbage was cooking and saw the lid of the saucepan rise and fall. 'Now let me think,' he murmured – 'let me think.' Then he struck his forehead and the steam engine was discovered. It was the same with me, although circumstances were rather different.

It was like this. Some years ago I spent a lot of time with a young lady who was very proud and conscious of being English. Once she asked me – to my great surprise – whether I would marry her. 'No,' I replied, 'I will not. My mother would never agree to my marrying a foreigner.' She looked at me a little surprised and irritated, and retorted: 'I, a foreigner? What a silly thing to say. I am English. You are the foreigner. And your mother, too.' I did not give in. 'In Budapest, too?' I asked her. 'Everywhere,' she declared with determination. 'Truth does not depend on geography. What is true in England is also true in Hungary and in North Borneo and Venezuela and everywhere.'

I saw that this truth was as irrefutable as it was simple. I was startled and upset. Mainly because of my mother whom I loved and respected. Now, I suddenly learned what she really was.

It was a shame and bad taste to be an alien, and it is no use pretending otherwise. There is no way out of it. A criminal may improve and become a decent member of society. A foreigner cannot improve. Once a foreigner, always a foreigner. There is no way out for him. He may become British; he can never become English.

(from *How to be an Alien* by George Mikes)

6 Write an imaginary letter home from an English or American immigrant who has been in your country for a year, saying what he/she likes, dislikes, finds easy and finds difficult.

All the Engish people are never foreiners

my mother has witish yeleow hare, pinkish eyes and lots of Teeth and she is very brtifull.

My Granny cries When she's happy and when she's sad She just stares.

My dad has Found a better mummy for us than the last one.

I've been marrid five times, mostly with my mother, but once I did get marrid to a girl who gave me some chewing gum, But that was on holiday.

My brother didn't want to get Married He wanted to take Me to Football

I want to Swop my Sister for Something better.

My brother looked horrible when was born but I didn't say so because they wouldn't let me change him.

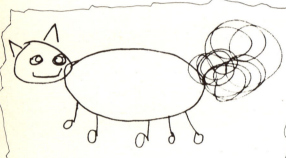

My Granddad says he doesnt like women So we bought Him a cat

My Sister and brother tell lyes it runs in the family

I was adopted so my parents wanted me very badly.

MY uncle has started to grow to Look Like a mouse.

(from *All Our Love, The Facts of Love, Lots of Love, The Best of Love* and *Vote for Love*, compiled by Nanette Newman)

Looking forward; looking back

A When you are old and grey

1 Grammar revision. Put in the right tenses.

1. When I .... an old woman I shall wear purple. (*be*)
2. Will you tell me as soon as the bell ....? (*ring*)
3. I'll be interested to see whether John .... tomorrow or not. (*come*)
4. After we've finished the building work, things .... easier. (*be*)
5. I'll have the letter finished before the postman .... here. (*get*)
6. I hope you .... me all about the holiday when you .... back. (*tell*; *get*)
7. Next time you come I .... you to see my mother. (*take*)
8. I don't know if I .... here when you .... tomorrow morning. (*be*; *phone*)

2 Grammar. Put in *shall* or *will*.

1. .... I help you with the cooking?
2. If I catch the 10.37 train, what time .... I be in London?
3. What .... I do with this book?
4. '.......... we go out for a drink this evening?' 'OK. Where .... we meet?'
5. Is the flight direct, or .... we have to change planes?
6. .... I be working next Saturday morning?
7. What .... I wear to Andy's party?
8. When .... we know the exam results?

3 Put in the future progressive or the future perfect.

1. What will you (*be doing/have done*) this time tomorrow?
2. How soon will the builders (*be finishing/have finished*) laying the foundations?
3. Do you think you'll (*be making/have made*) a decision by next July?
4. Next Sunday morning I'll (*be sitting/have sat*) on a beach doing nothing.
5. By the end of the year I'll .... 20,000 miles on business. (*drive*)
6. We'll .... for you at the station when you arrive. (*wait*)
7. Jennie and I .... here for twenty years next September. (*be*)
8. I think when I'm 80 I'll probably still .... to understand what goes on in your head. (*try*)

4 Say when you *will*, *may* or *might* do some of the following things. Use some or all of the expressions in the box.

```
soon    one day    one of these days
sometime    sooner or later    never
```

learn Russian/Chinese/Japanese/Latin/...
learn the piano/violin/trumpet/...
travel to Australia/Canada/India...
take up jogging/parachuting/hang-gliding/...
write a novel/play/short story/...
take a long holiday
get married (again) / have (more) children / get divorced
give up smoking/drinking/gambling/...

5 Read the poems with a dictionary.

FIRE AND ICE

Some say the world will end in fire,
Some say in ice.
From what I've tasted of desire
I hold with those who favour fire.
But if it had to perish twice,
I think I know enough of hate
To say that for destruction ice
Is also great
And would suffice.

(Robert Frost)

HEAVEN

The god-men say when die go sky
Through pearly gates where river flow,
The god-men say when die we fly
Just like eagle, hawk and crow.
Might be, might be –
But I don't know.

(Australian aborigine's comment on Christianity)

NEW YEAR RESOLUTIONS

This year
I shall lock next year in a cupboard
with last year
and feed them on bread and water.

This year
I shall let in
what is worth letting in only
(but for that
my door is wide open).

This year
earth and air
fire and water
will be welcome at my breakfast table
(and so will you).

This year
I shall amass the world's largest collection
of unburst soap-bubbles.

This year
the rain and I
will dance together
on several occasions.

This year
I shall change the world with a poem.

This year
I shall give you starring roles
in many of my dreams.

This year
dogs that chase me
while I am out jogging
will wish they hadn't.
(I refuse to give details
for security reasons.)

This year
I shall chat up all my wrong numbers
and make new friends.

This year
I shall teach the baby to dance
and play poker.

This year
I shall find the end of the rainbow
dig up the pot of gold
and buy dresses for you
and jewellery
(and you shall have the rainbow for your hair
and the crescent moon
as a pendant).

(Lewis Mancha)

6 Add a verse or two of your own to the poem 'New Year Resolutions'.

134

B I wish we'd never met

1 Grammar: tenses after *I wish* and *If only*. Put in the right tenses.

1. I wish I .... speak more languages. (*can*)
2. If only I .... what she was thinking! (*know*)
3. Don't you wish you .... a sweater like this? (*have*)
4. I wish weekends .... more often. (*come*)
5. If only it .... so cold we could go for a walk. (*not be*)
6. I wish I .... a cat – it must be a nice life. (*be*)
7. I wish I .... my exams when I was at school. (*pass*)
8. Do you ever wish you .... born? (*not be*)
9. If only I .... smoking! (*not start*)
10. I wish I .... never .... you. (*meet*)
11. I wish I .... my money on something else instead of buying that car. (*spend*)

2 Pronunciation. Copy the words and underline the stressed syllables.

attitude   bilingual   birthplace   community
continually   extended   fluently   generation
immediate   increasingly   isolation
limited   memory   occupy   overcrowded
positive   preserve   refugee   relation
stubborn   surprising

3 At the moment you are probably spending a lot of your time studying English. What could you have decided to do with the time instead? Write at least five sentences, using the structure *I could have* ... + past participle. Examples:

I could have studied mathematics.
I could have built a boat.

4 You probably didn't do everything that you should have done yesterday, last weekend, last week or last year. Write at least five sentences about things that you should have done but didn't, using the structure *I should have* ... + past participle. Examples:

I should have phoned my father yesterday.
I should have cleaned the car on Sunday.

5 Vocabulary revision. Write the names of all the vegetables in the picture. Can you add the names of five more vegetables?

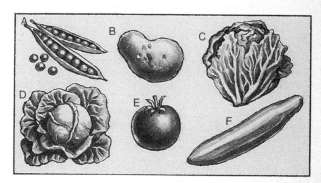

6 Read the poem with a dictionary.

CONVERSATIONS WITH MY FAIRY GODMOTHER

I

You deaf cow.
I said bold, not bald.
You can forget the other three wishes.

II

'Hello, Fairy Godmother. You again.'

'Hello, son.
I'll give you a choice.
Twenty pounds now
or you can be recognised after your death
as the greatest poet of the century.'

'Make it twenty-five.'

III

'So that's the baby.'

'It is indeed,
Fairy Godmother.'

'Very nice.
Would you prefer it to have beauty
or intelligence
or fame?'

'Gosh
Fairy Godmother
can we think it over?'

'Or regular meals?'

(H. Highwater)

7 Here are some parts of a story. Can you invent the missing parts and write out the complete story?

A VISIT FROM MY FAIRY GODMOTHER
I had a visit from my fairy godmother yesterday evening. I looked up from my newspaper, and there she was standing by the window.

'Hello,' she said. 'I'm your fairy godmother.' She didn't look quite as I expected. ....

....

'What do you want?' I asked.
'Well,' she said. 'I've come to give you three wishes. That's what fairy godmothers do. They give you three wishes, don't they? What's your first wish?'
'OK,' I said. 'I'd like ....
......................................,'

'That's a bit of an unusual wish,' she said. 'I don't think I've ever heard that one before. Anyway, if that's what you want –'

....

'Actually,' I said, 'I think that wish was a bit of a mistake. I'm sorry I wished that wish. Can I have my next one?'
'OK,' she said. 'What is it?'

....

'Are you sure?' she asked.

....

'Right,' I said. 'That was much more satisfactory. Now for my last wish, ...

....

'That's going to be a bit difficult to manage,' she said. 'But I'll see what I can do.'

....

'Well, thanks for everything,' I said. 'Is there anything you'd like before you go?'

....

8 Write a story about a visit from your fairy godmother.

"In all my years as a fairy, that's the silliest use of three wishes I've ever seen."

THERE IS NO PRACTICE BOOK WORK FOR UNIT 30

136

Answers to Exercises

Unit 1, Lesson B

3

1. Some common verbs which are followed by an -ing form are: *avoid, can't help, dislike, enjoy, feel like, finish, imagine, (don't) mind, suggest.*
2. Some common verbs which are followed by an infinitive with *to* are: *agree, ask, begin, decide, forget, happen, learn, manage, seem.*

Unit 4, Lesson B

7

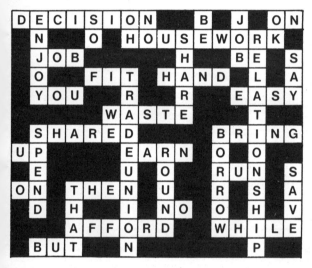

Unit 6, Lesson B

2

Say and tell

Tell is usually followed by a personal direct object; *say* is normally used without a personal object. Compare:

I *told her* that it was important.
I *said* that it was important.
(OR I *said* to her that it was important.)

Unit 8, Lesson B

7

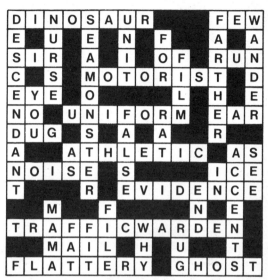

Unit 12, Lesson B

7

Unit 15, Lesson B
7

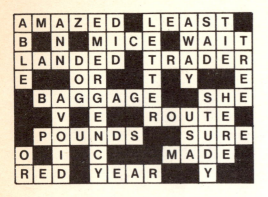

Unit 18, Lesson B
8

Unit 22, Lesson A
1
Rule 3 is correct.

Unit 22, Lesson B
6

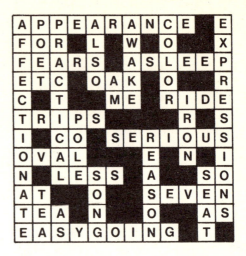

Unit 25, Lesson B
4
Bill broke the window. Everyone else was named as the guilty party at least once, and since everyone was lying, it must have been Bill. Also, Bill was lying when he said it wasn't him.

Unit 26, Lesson B
5

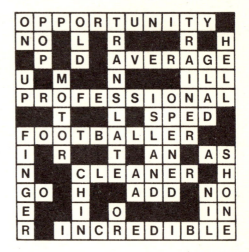

Acknowledgements

The authors and publishers are grateful to the following copyright owners for permission to reproduce photographs, illustrations and texts. Every endeavour has been made to contact copyright owners and apologies are expressed for any omissions.

page 5: 'What is he?' by D.H. Lawrence from *The Complete Poems of D.H. Lawrence*, collected and edited by Vivian de Sola Pinto and F. Warren Roberts. Copyright © 1964, 1971 by Angelo Ravagli and C.M. Weekley, executors of the Estate of Frieda Lawrence Ravagli. Reprinted by permission of Viking Penguin, Inc. and Laurence Pollinger Ltd. 'Mrs Webb' from *Loneliness* by Jeremy Seabrook reprinted by permission of the author. page 13: 'Tree talk...' by Thomas O'Toole and 'A new branch...' by Anthony Tucker reprinted by permission of *The Guardian*. page 15: 'Commuter who talks...' reprinted by permission of *The Evening Standard*. 'What are his intentions?' taken from the 'Dear Abby' column, by Abigail Van Buren. Copyright 1985, Universal Press Syndicate. Reprinted with permission. All rights reserved. 'First US city...' reprinted by permission of I. Wallace, D. Wallechinsky, A. Wallace, 'Significa' and *Parade*. page 18: Excerpts reprinted by permission of Grosset & Dunlap from *Isaac Asimov's Book of Facts*, copyright © 1979 by Red Dembner Enterprises Corp. page 21: Advertisement reproduced by permission of Epson (UK) Ltd, Cogent Elliot Ltd and Kevin Baldwin. page 23: *br* Reproduced by permission of The Advertising Standards Authority. page 30: 'Prison cell forgery...' (31 July 1975) and 'Prisoner's night out...' by Richard Ford (27 October 1980) reprinted by permission of Times Newspapers Ltd. 'Good excuse...' and 'Fag end...' reprinted by permission of United Press International Ltd. page 32: From *Curious Facts* by John May reprinted by permission of Martin Secker & Warburg and Holt, Rinehart and Winston, Inc. page 35: From *Darkness at Noon* by Arthur Koestler adapted by permission of the Estate of Arthur Koestler, Jonathan Cape Ltd and A.D. Peters & Co. Ltd. page 38: From *The Unsafe Sky* by William Norris reprinted by permission of the author. page 41: 'Pilot holds New York hostage' adapted by permission of Jane Rosen and *The Guardian*. 'Chipmunk lands...' adapted by permission of John Hooper and *The Guardian*. 'The train not stopping...' adapted by permission of *The Oxford Times*. page 44: Extracts from *The Piccolo Explorer Book of Mysteries*, copyright Grisewood & Dempsey Ltd, London. page 65: Excerpt from *Eating and Allergy* by Robert Eagle. Copyright © 1980 by Robert Eagle. Reprinted by permission of Doubleday, a division of Bantam, Doubleday, Dell Publishing Group, Inc. and A.P. Watt Ltd. Excerpt from *Fears and Phobias* by Dr Tony Whitehead adapted by permission of Sheldon Press. 'First Day at School' from *In the Glassroom* by Roger McGough reprinted by permission of Jonathan Cape Ltd and A.D. Peters & Co. Ltd. page 67: From 'Snip, Prune and Slide' by Clive Ponting abridged by permission of the author and *The New Statesman*. page 69: Quotations from 'This England' column reprinted by permission of *The New Statesman*. page 74: From *Black Boy* by Richard Wright reprinted by permission of Mrs Ellen Wright and Jonathan Cape Ltd. Copyright 1937, 1942, 1944, 1945 by Richard Wright. Reprinted by permission of Harper & Row, Publishers, Inc. page 80: 'Stopping by woods on a snowy evening' by Robert Frost. Copyright 1923, © 1969 by Holt, Rinehart and Winston, Inc. Copyright 1951 by Robert Frost. Reprinted from *The Poetry of Robert Frost* edited by Edward Connery Lathem, by permission of Henry Holt and Company, Inc. and Jonathan Cape Ltd. 'Curaçao' from *The Bear on the Delhi Road* by Earle Birney reprinted by permission of Chatto and Windus Ltd. Used by permission of the Canadian Publishers, McClelland and Stewart, Toronto. page 82: From *Parkinson's Law* by C. Northcote Parkinson reprinted by permission of John Murray (Publishers) Ltd. page 86: Adapted by permission from *War on Want General Secretary's Report*. page 88: 'Good food...' by Alex Finer (16 November 1975) reprinted by permission of Times Newspapers Ltd. 'When even the price...' reprinted by permission of J. McGregor-Davies. page 98: 'The day...' adapted by permission of *The Oxford Times*. page 103: 'Lily Smalls' by Dylan Thomas, *Under Milk Wood*. Copyright 1954 by New Directions Publishing Corporation. Reprinted by permission of David Higham Associates Ltd. 'The Translator' from *Siege of Silence* by A.J. Quinnell reprinted by permission of Hodder and Stoughton Ltd and Sandal A.G., Switzerland. 'Bookrest' from *Codeword Cromwell* by Ted Allbeury reprinted by permission of Grafton Books – a division of the Collins Publishing Group. 'Prehistoric woman' from *The Clan of the Cave Bear*. Copyright 1980 by Jean M. Auel. Published by Crown Publishers Inc. Used by permission. Reprinted by permission of Hodder and Stoughton Ltd.   page 110: From 'Why men make rotten patients' by Dr Vernon Coleman reprinted by permission of the author.   page 111: From *The Complete Poems of Carl Sandburg*, copyright 1950 by Carl Sandburg; renewed 1978 by Margaret Sandburg, Helga Sandburg Crile and Janet Sandburg. Reprinted by permission of Harcourt Brace Jovanovich, Inc.   page 114: From *You Have Been Warned* by Fougasse and McCullogh reprinted by permission of Methuen & Co.   page 115: Extracts from *I Want to Know What's in My File* reprinted by permission of The Campaign for Freedom of Information.   page 118: From *How to be an Alien* by George Mikes reprinted by permission of André Deutsch. From 'How do they know – why do we lie?' by Russell Baker reprinted by permission of *The International Herald Tribune*.   page 128: 'Days' reprinted by permission of Faber and Faber Ltd from *The Whitsun Weddings* by Philip Larkin.   page 130: From *Dreaming in a Foreign Language* by Carol Rumens reprinted by permission of the author.   page 131: From *How to be an Alien* by George Mikes reprinted by permission of André Deutsch.   page 134: 'Fire and ice' by Robert Frost. Copyright 1923, © 1969 by Holt, Rinehard and Winston, Inc. Copyright 1951 by Robert Frost. Reprinted from *The Poetry of Robert Frost* edited by Edward Connery Lathem, by permission of Henry Holt and Company, Inc. and Jonathan Cape Ltd. Reproduced by permission of *Punch*: pages 4 *tr*; 6 *b*; 7 *tl*; 9 *tr*; 10 *b*; 11 *tl, tr*; 13 *t*; 14 *bl*; 15 *tr*; 19 *tl*; 26 *t*; 27 *tr, b*; 33 *bl*; 37 *t*; 43 *tl*; 44 *tr*; 46 *b*; 48 *br*; 49 *br*; 54 *bl*; 55 *cr*, 56 *br*; 60 *b*; 62 *br*; 63 *b*; 64 *bl*; 68 *cl, cr*; 71 *bl, br*; 78 *bc*; 82 *tr*; 84 *br*; 96 *tl, tr, c*; 96 *b*; 100 *br*; 102 *br*; 103 *b*; 105 *b*; 108 *tl, tr, cl, cr*; 109 *bl*; 110 *b*; 112 *tr, cl, cr, bl, br*; 114 *br*; 116 *tr*; 118 *cr, br*; 121 *b*; 123 *c*; 127 *br*; 128 *tr*; 134 *tr*; 136 *b*.   Reproduced by permission of *The Observer*: page 5 *b*. Reproduced by permission of Syndication International (1986) Ltd: pages 8 *tr*, 82 *br*. Reproduced by permission of Victorama Ltd: pages 36 *b*, 42 *tr*.   Reproduced by permission of P. Cleveland-Peck: page 50 *tr*.   Reproduced by permission of *Weekend Magazine*: page 66 *tr*. Reproduced by permission of Morris Jones: page 62 *tr*.   Extracts from *Vote for Love* © Bryan Forbes Ltd 1978, published by Collins: pages 69, 93, 132.   Extracts from *Lots of Love* © Bryan Forbes Ltd 1974, published by Collins: pages 74, 93, 132.   Extracts from *The Facts of Love* © Bryan Forbes Ltd 1980, published by Collins: pages 74, 132.   Reproduced by permission of Compass News Features: page 91.   Extracts from *God Bless Love* © Invalid Children's Aid Association 1984, published by Collins: page 93.   From *Some Damn Fool Signed The Rubens Again* by Norman Thelwell, reproduced by permission of Methuen, London: page 99.   Reproduced by permission of Shelter: page 101. Reproduced by permission of Citroën and Colman RSCG: page 114 *tr*.   Extracts from *All our Love* © Bryan Forbes Ltd 1978 and *The Best of Love* © Bryan Forbes Ltd 1985, published by Collins: page 132.

Joe McEwan, pages 16, 28 *t* and *b*, 44 *b*, 45, 64 *r*, 79 *b*, 81, 83 *l* and *r*, 84 *bl*, 94, 106, 124, 135;   Banks and Miles, pages 58, 84 *cr*, 104, 113;   Sue Hitchens, pages 9 *b*, 117;   Maria Richer, pages 29, 72, 96 *br*; Wendy Jones (John Craddock Agency), pages 20, 35.

(Abbreviations: t = top b = bottom c = centre r = right l = left)